The Great American Road Trip

Roam the Roads From Coast to Coast

gestalten

Embrace the Freedom of the Open Road

Discover 25 routes that will bring you closer to nature, others, and yourself.

A long drive can reveal the threads that comprise a nation's fabric. Get on the road and discover how America was weaved, where its myths unravel, which narratives endure, and the values that continue to hold it together—all the while adding your own story to the national library.

What distinguishes those who drive long distances for pleasure is that they are most alive when on the road. They take off for days, weeks, or even months at a time, delighting their palates, gaining new perspectives, and getting a deeper understanding of their nation. These are just the side effects, by the way, and you don't get them from just leaving one place and landing neatly in another. In all that in-between, many will, for the first time, not just look at their country but actually see it. And whatever may be said about that slippery notion known as freedom, the all-American virtue, you'll certainly find more of it on the road than in the static scenery of your habitual existence.

Most of us, in our relationship with the road, are commuters first and travelers second. But this is changing and has been for a while. The pandemic has only accelerated the road trip's renaissance. Get in and go—that's it, that's all. It is with this attitude that more and more people are discovering that the real value of a long drive is not getting anywhere in particular but getting away in general, both spiritually and spatially. In each respect, it is also about getting closer to yourself, others, nature, and those ancient, changeless rhythms: sunup, sundown; tide in, tide out; inhale, exhale.

The novelist James T. Farrell once observed that "America is so vast that almost everything said about it is likely to be true, and the opposite is probably equally true." These pages are an attempt to map this vastness—not just geographically but also culturally, historically, and culinarily—so you can find your own truth. Taste your way through Texas or Maine, ride the waves of California or the slopes of Colorado, and retrace the footsteps of those who have traversed the land. Discover the modern marvels of Connecticut, walk on scorched earth, and see what's up in Alaska. Visit and explore national parks. Feel the blues, stargaze, step out of your car and into the sea. Leave your comfort zone, expand your horizons, chase skies, or just observe ordinary life in another context as poet Geoffrey Hills suggests: "This is plenty. This is more than enough."

Inevitably, getting closer to all these wonderful places and meditations will also bring you closer to others. Sit down with them at one table, spend a night in their homes, hear their stories. You'll encounter alternative ways of living, thinking, and looking out towards the world. This is the most valuable education available to us, and on the road, it exists in abundance. All you have to do is keep your eyes wide and your mind open.

Now, as veterans of the road know, the best experiences always occur as "happy little accidents." Which is why we encourage you to take the itineraries in this book as a guide and not gospel. Remain imprecise and improvise, like a chef cooking to taste. Know that a wrong turn can lead to the right kind of nowhere, the type of place where relatively few people care a lot about something largely insignificant. To be on the road is to be adrift with possibility. Anything can happen and the only guarantees are uncertainty and surprise—and of course the wonder that ensues when you combine the two.

The Call of the Open Road

Leave routine in the rearview, buckle up, and venture into the unknown.

We have embarked on countless road trips, some meticulously planned, others last minute and rogue, but all of them documented, the camera forever commemorating the memories made. We've ridden our motorcycles or gotten behind the wheel to traverse the jaw-dropping scapes of Alaska, the jagged vistas of the Rocky Mountains,

and the sweeping plains of the California desert, to name only a few of the places we've ventured. We have taken four wheels—and oftentimes two—across more state lines than we can recall, and the stories they have left us with are something we will never forget. The open road has humbled us and been our teacher; it's expanded our minds and opened our eyes. It has sparked our creativity and exhausted us beyond measure. And it always calls us back.

Naturally, there have been some wrong turns. We've gotten chased off private land in Colorado. (To be clear, we didn't know we were on private land until we were being run off of it.) We have fallen off our bikes on long and technical rides, damaging both our bodies and our egos. We have made our way down Beartooth Highway along the Montana-Wyoming border, one of the

most epic and beautiful roads in the country (see pp. 165, 169). We have camped on the edge of the Grand Canyon in a spot so secluded we wouldn't know how to get back to if we tried. But isn't that the magic of a good road trip? The burger at that side-of-the-road restaurant in some tiny town you can't totally picture. The gorgeous vista from a road you didn't see on the map. The stories you never imagined sharing but after so many hours on the road, nothing feels off-limits.

If the last few years have taught us anything it's that the road can offer respite in times of uncertainty. When the world seems to be falling apart and taking to the air isn't an option, there is always a way to weave through this great country of ours; there is always a new place to see, a wrong turn yet to be made. And sometimes those unmapped journeys lead to the best

Spend enough time on the road and you'll begin to understand it isn't really about arriving anywhere or even getting away from it all. These are mere inevitabilities. The real project at hand is to get closer to yourself and the stories we tell ourselves.

destinations—and they most *certainly* make for the best stories. As our AETHER mantra states, "You Only Get One Spin," so you better make it a good one. As owners of an adventure-clothing brand, we always have our sights set on where to go next, what new place we can discover, what parts of this country we have yet to explore. A good road trip can excite and enlighten. It can change your perspective, the way you view the world. That's why working with gestalten on this book appealed to us. We aim to live lives full of exploration and spontaneous journeys—one where routine is cast aside in favor of the unknown. The following pages tell some of those stories: sit down, buckle up, and enjoy the ride.

Jonah Smith & Palmer West,
co-founders, AETHER

Taste Test Your Way along the Maine Lobster Trail

BOSTON, MASSACHUSETTS →
BAR HARBOR, MAINE →
PORTLAND, MAINE

Welcome to Maine, where things run on Lobster Time. What does that mean? Hit the road and find out.

The lobster roll is a simple dish, really: fresh tail and claw meat served on a hot dog-style bun and seasoned with lemon, salt, pepper, and butter. As for who does it best—why not find out for yourself?

The biggest rivalry on the Eastern Seaboard isn't between Boston's Bruins and Montreal's Canadiens but between the lobsters of Maine and Atlantic Canada. Let's just say, for the sake of argument, that the superior specimens come from the waters of Maine. Well, then we arrive at the next heated debate: where in the state can you eat the best lobster? This road trip is designed so you can find out for yourself.

In terms of timing, it's best to go when the lobsters are most active. That means somewhere between the end of June and December, though most restaurants (or *shacks,* in local parlance) board up for the winter. Try to time your trip to coincide with Indian summer, when the foliage turns to inferno. The journey starts in Boston, makes its way to Bar Harbor, and concludes in Portland—around 475 miles (764 kilometers) not including impromptu detours. Plan for about a week.

So, Boston. Start strong with a breakfast lobster roll at Pauli's, which is just a few blocks from the bay and was honored by Guy Fieri in *Diners, Drive-ins, and Dives* in 2020. Then it's time to hit the road for the longest stretch of the trip, to Rockland. Break it up around halfway with a stop in Kennebunkport, a small coastal town that's about as Maine as it gets. Just look at the names of the restaurants: The Boathouse, Pier 77, Arundel Wharf, Mabel's Lobster Claw, Cape Pier Chowder House, Hurricane Restaurant. Work up an appetite by taking a stroll along Gooch's Beach and around Cape Arundel toward Blowing Cave Park. You'll find the heart of the town's lobster heritage a couple miles up the coast, in Cape Porpoise, where Nunan's coastal

classics will hold you over on the remainder of the drive to Rockland, Maine. I-95N and US-1N will both get you there. The former is quicker, but the latter allows you to explore various towns en route. You can combine the two depending on your mood and time constraints.

Rockland is a great gateway to the hundreds of inlets and coves dotting the area's coastline. Once there, switch up your wheels and see the Penobscot Bay area by bike. The Rockland Breakwater Lighthouse is a worthy sight if you're into sea beacons, as is Jess's Market, with its counter full of daily catches. For off-the-boat take-home lobster, meanwhile, look no further than J&J's. Or have the pros take care of dinner by booking a table at North Beacon Oyster, lest you think being around water and eating things

that live in it is all there is to do around here. Rockland is just a stone's throw from Ragged Mountain and its plentiful hikes and lakes. Driving the interior roads evokes simpler times, whatever they may mean for you, and is bound to reveal treasures at every turn. Case in point: Oyster River Winegrowers. We'll spare the details—just go and treat your taste buds.

From Rockland, it's a little over two hours on US-1N to Bar Harbor. Consider a stopover in Belfast to stretch your legs. There you can get your no-fuss lobster fix at Young's Lobster Pound, or if you skipped breakfast, see what's baking at Crumbs Provisions. For Bar Harbor, plan at least two days since there's not just the town to explore but all of Mount Desert Island. Don't be afraid to drive around rather aimlessly. →

In terms of timing, it's best to go when the lobsters are most active, between the end of June and December. Try to time your trip to coincide with Indian summer, when the foliage turns to inferno.

Rockland is known as the Lobster Capital of the World. No surprise, then, that it also has its own annual lobster festival. You'll find no shortage of seafood fare at the small town's more than 50 restaurants, including the legendary Claw.

→ There aren't too many roads, and stumbling upon something spectacular is all but guaranteed—the lobster mac and cheese at The Travelin Lobster, for example, or a scrumptious homemade pie from Mount Dessert Bakery. Back in town, indulge in a fresh local brew at Fogtown, and stop by Ben and Bill's Chocolate Emporium for something truly unhinged: lobster ice cream. Finally, save some time for nature. Sand Beach, Acadia National Park, and Conners Nubble are enough to satisfy any yearning for the great outdoors.

Heading back down the coast, make a stop in Wiscasset on your way to Boothbay. Wiscasset is known almost exclusively as the home of Red's Eats, an absolute A-lister among lobster shacks. The line can be long but is always worth it. Boothbay is just as buzzing and for good reason. With its bustling harbor, movie-scene cafes, and wharf architecture, it's the kind of town you put on a postcard.

The lighthouse is a worthy sight if you're into sea beacons.

Sail with the Bennie Alice from Pier 6 in Boothbay Harbor to Cabbage Island on a scenic cruise along Maine's coastline. Upon arrival, indulge in a traditional Downeast clambake. You basically step off the boat and into the kitchen—can't miss it.

The last leg of the road trip takes you from Boothbay to Portland with a quick pull over in Freeport. When you get there, drive through the main drag and make a beeline for Harraseeket Lunch & Lobster, whose extensive menu will please any and all appetites. Walk around a little to build your hunger up again because you'll need it for Portland, Maine. It is the biggest city and, therefore, also the one with the highest concentration of lobster restaurants. Eventide Oyster Co. puts a fun twist on the classic roll with its Chinese-style steamed bun, while you'll find an equally inventive range of seafood fare at Scales. And if by the end of the trip you feel like there's something you missed, just remember: the next lobster season is only a year away. ◆

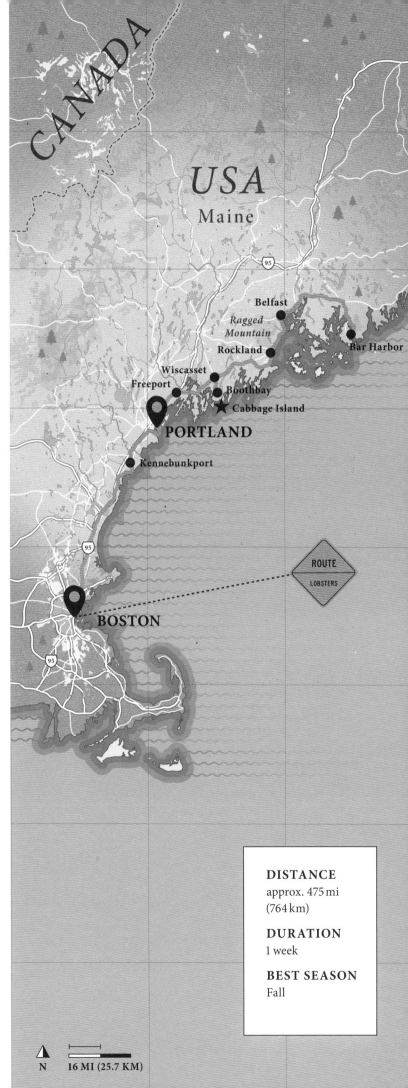

DISTANCE
approx. 475 mi
(764 km)

DURATION
1 week

BEST SEASON
Fall

Follow the Foliage:
A Deciduous Journey
From Green to Gold

KEENE VALLEY, NEW YORK → BAR HARBOR, MAINE

The trees are alive with color in the northeastern
states, and this route shows off the full spectrum.

Fall in the northeastern states is a magical time of the year. Nature begins a dramatic changing of the guard, a colorful reimagining of the woodland canvas as the banks of trees slowly change color. People travel in droves to witness the majesty of this annual process; the "leaf peepers," as they're known, make an aesthetic pilgrimage to revel in the rich tapestry.

This 475-mile (764-kilometer) route slices across the northeastern corner of the United States, beginning in the relative wilderness of the Keene Valley. Known as the High Peaks Region, the town is flanked by some of the highest and most majestic mountains in the Adirondacks, all peppered with hiking trails and world-class climbing routes hewn into the rugged landscape. Birch trees stretch as far as the eye can see as you drive east along US-9N toward the shores of Lake Champlain.

The yellows, oranges, and reds of the beech, birch, and maple trees create a polychromatic glow in the fall sun.

It's quite something to look back on the road behind you as you board the Essex-Charlotte ferry at sunset (or sunrise), and there are spectacular views of the foliage that blankets the Adirondack and Green Mountains. Thirty minutes later, you're disembarking in Vermont, and 30 minutes after that, you've arrived in Burlington. The beauty of this region is that it should stir your culinary appetites as well as your visual ones, and a short jaunt down I-89 lands you at the doorstep of everyone's favorite ice cream factory, Ben & Jerry's.

Ice cream is just one of the regional specialties that will have you making refueling stops as you glide past the golden leaves of Vermont's beech and birch trees. Cold Hollow Cider Mill as you leave Waterbury Village on Route 100 is one such place of respite; the mantra here whisking you away from the responsibilities of the outside world: apples, bees, and maple trees. Savor the tart warmth of their delicious cider or the gummy sweetness of their homemade maple

The so-called "Indian summer," a period of unseasonably warm, dry weather in late October or November, lures foliage fans from around the world to the northeastern corner of the United States. Sleepy Hollow Farm is an especially charming place to take in the colors.

syrup. These are the flavors of fall, evocative and reassuring, and you'll find any number of independent artisans along the way.

Heading north to Stowe, Vermont, the road is nestled between the Mount Mansfield and CC Putnam State Forests, the hillsides ablaze with color from mid-September into late October. You can unexpectedly fulfill your Sound of Music fantasies as you pass or even stay at the Trapp Family Lodge, an Austrian-inspired mountain resort that has been in operation since 1950 by a real-life Von Trapp family (that is, they share a name with the family from the movie and were even known as the Trapp Family Singers before they changed careers). If blasting "Climb Every Mountain" from the car isn't cheesy enough, an hour along VT-15 lands you on the Cabot Cheese Farm, where you can load up on cheddar and pepper jack for snacking under the glorious surrounding canopies.

I-93 winds its twisted way through the verdant Vermont countryside, across another state border, and into New Hampshire. The vibrant peaks of Mount Lafayette and Mount Lincoln appear, towering as they do into the alpine zone, where only dwarf vegetation pokes through. The mountains are surrounded by the abundant beauty of Franconia Notch State Park, though, with the yellows, oranges, and reds of the beech, birch, and maple trees creating a polychromatic glow in the fall sun.

The displays continue on as you meet US-302E, which loops south through the White Mountain National Forest and the Attitash Mountain Resort. It's a good opportunity to leave the sanctuary of your car and let the train take the strain for a while. The Conway Scenic Railway leaves from the gorgeously preserved North Conway Railway Station, a Victorian edifice dating back to 1874. The 1920s–1950s-era passenger cars whisk you through the forests, your eyes free to take in the views and your hands free to snap photos as the colors fly past.

As you head north along NH-16 through the foothills of Mount Washington and then joining US-2E, you'll cross another state line, this time into Maine. The leaves are still the prime attraction, but the wildlife of Grafton Notch State Park, just north of Bethel, is a close second in terms of sightseeing. There are hikes of varying difficulty in the picturesque →

Vermont is known for four things: maple syrup, cheddar cheese, Ben & Jerry's, and Bernie Sanders. And while you probably won't run across the senator during your road trip, you should absolutely seek out everything else on the list.

→ mountains of the Mahoosuc Range, and birdwatchers can often see peregrine falcons and a wide variety of songbirds. Deer, bears, and grouse go about their business in the lower slopes, and the trout in the park's rivers attract fishing aficionados from far and wide.

The slight southeastern track down toward Augusta, Maine, slowly sees woodland give way to lakes. The shores of the Androscoggin and Maranacook Lakes can be seen from the road as you drive along ME-133E and the Androscoggin Riverlands State Park is a lovely spot to stretch cramped legs. The relatively flat 10 miles (16 kilometers) of nature trails snake into the woods, white pines, cedars, and fir trees coming into the mix. More alpine ambiance can be found at the Matterhorn Ski Bar in Newry, a cozy cabin

with a wood-fired oven and a welcome for weary travelers.

The Atlantic Ocean draws ever nearer as you drive along US-1N and ME-3E toward the final stop of Bar Harbor, Maine. Small towns and villages start to come thick and fast, the blue waters of Penobscot Bay jutting into the increasingly jagged coastline. As your destination approaches, so does the expanse of the Acadia National Park, the highest rocky headlands of the Atlantic coast. Don't think the adventure is over, as the park has 27 miles (43 kilometers) of historic motor roads and some 160 miles (257 kilometers) of hiking trails. It's a fitting spot for a last look at the fall colors, the park cloaked in spruce-fir forest, with oak, maple, and beech adding to the backdrop. After a

final hike, it's time to relax and fill up on Maine lobster or a warming bowl of chowder.

The landscapes painted by nature will stay with you as winter takes hold, the colors still fresh in your mind, the coziness of the New England landscape keeping you warm even as the leaves fall. It's one of the natural world's most spectacular shows, and the more time you take to appreciate it, the longer those memories will remain. ◆

CANADA

Montreal

87

LAKE CHAMPLAIN

Mount Mansfield
State Forest

15

Essex-Charlotte ferry

Burlington

Stowe

CC Putnam
State Forest

Cabot Cheese farm

89

Waterbury

93

Mount Lafayette
(5,249 ft)

9

White Moun
National F

KEENE VALLEY

Adirondack
Mountains

Franconia Notch
State Park

Mount Lincoln
(5,089 ft)

Attit
Moun
Res

87

New York

91

Vermont

New Hampshire

91

N   6 MI (9.7 KM)

DISTANCE
approx. 475 mi
(764 km)

DURATION
1 week

BEST SEASON
Fall

USA
Maine

95

Grafton Notch
State Park

2

ANDROSCOGGIN
LAKE

MARANACOOK LAKE

1

BAR HARBOR

Bethel

ROUTE

LEAF
FOLIAGE

Acadia
National
Park

Androscoggin
Riverlands
State Park

Augusta

th Conway
way Station

295

GULF OF MAINE

Marvel at Modern Connecticut

NEW CANAAN, CONNECTICUT →
HARTFORD, CONNECTICUT

Take a road trip back to the future and discover how an international movement took hold in small-town New England.

Perhaps in no other state can one more strongly feel the tugging of America's past while being propelled by tomorrow's promise. This juxtaposition plays out most admirably in Connecticut's architecture, from stately halls and manors to the modern marvels guiding this three-day itinerary from New Canaan through New Haven to Hartford. See what we mean? Even the names of towns grapple with shuffles of time. No wonder being here can feel like going back to the future.

It goes without saying that this route is best enjoyed behind the wheel of a DeLorean. Should you not have one on hand, any vehicle will do—as will any time of year. And with so much to see indoors, this is a truly winter-friendly road trip.

The arrival of the "Harvard Five"—Philip Johnson, Marcel Breuer, Landis Gores, John M. Johansen, and Eliot Noyes—put New Canaan at the center of the modern design movement in the early 1940s. Around 60 buildings from that era are still standing today.

Just hit the road and see what you stumble upon— there's more than enough modernism to marvel at.

But first, let's cozy up with a quick recap of how modernism took hold in this corner of New England. The movement actually has its roots in the Bauhaus school, which ended abruptly in its native Germany when the Nazi Party came to power. One of its principal emigrants, the designer Marcel Breuer, would settle in Cambridge, Massachusetts, where he became an instructor at the Harvard Graduate School of Design. Fueled by postwar optimism, Breuer and four of his students—John M. Johansen, Landis Gores, Philip Johnson, and Eliot Noyes—chose New Canaan as the canvas on which to bring their future-forward concepts to life. They would come to be known as the Harvard Five.

And so we begin there, in New Canaan. The town is home to at least 50 seminal modern residences, none more iconic than Johnson's Glass House. Looking at it, one can't help but recall the proverb about those who shouldn't throw stones. Other notable abodes in the vicinity include the Gores Pavilion at Irwin Park, the Mills House, Breuer House 1, and the Rantoul House. Not all of the original gems are listed or visible, so be sure to do some research before setting off. Or just hit the road and see what you stumble upon—there's more than enough modernism to marvel at. Finally, don't pass up a stop at Grace Farms with its modernist mission of harnessing an "intentionally designed space to communicate a set of values and advance good in the world for years to come."

Next, it's on to Stamford, a 20-minute jaunt southwest of New Canaan. Don't miss its delightfully puzzling Fish Church, which serves as the town's Presbyterian house of worship. Designed by architect Wallace K. Harrison and completed in 1958, the building is flooded with colorful light when the sun hits its stained glass "scales." Finish day one by lodging up at the GrayBarns, a 19th-century estate that's been revivified as a boutique hotel. For dinner, see what's on the menu at the in-house tavern or →

Don't pass up a stop
at Grace Farms,
with its modernist mission
"to communicate a
set of values and advance
good in the world for
years to come."

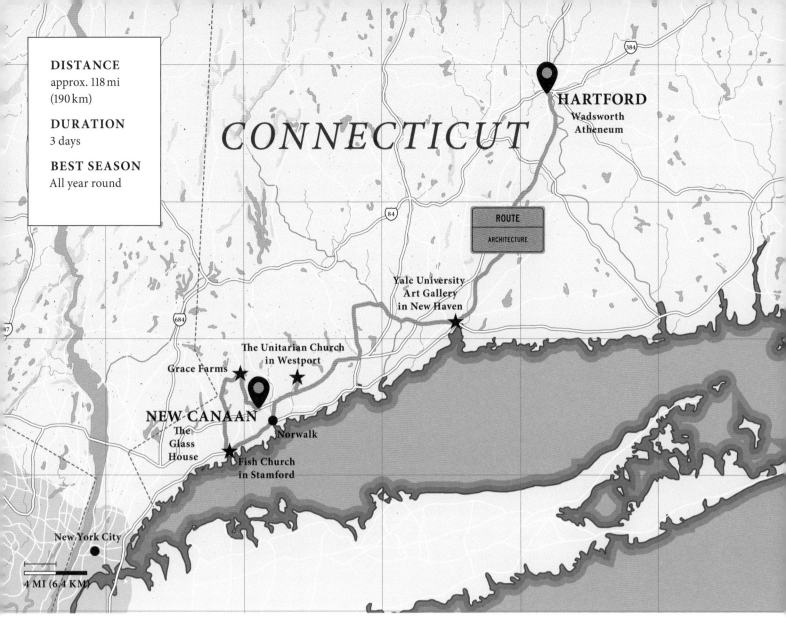

CONNECTICUT

HARTFORD
Wadsworth
Atheneum

ROUTE

ARCHITECTURE

Yale University
Art Gallery
in New Haven

The Unitarian Church
in Westport

Grace Farms

NEW CANAAN
The
Glass
House

Norwalk

Fish Church
in Stamford

New York City

4 MI (6.4 KM)

Philip Johnson's Glass House is probably the most famous of Connecticut's modern marvels. The American architect lived in the house from 1949 until his death in 2005. Today, visitors can book tours of the building and surrounding property.

→ head to Oak and Almond in Norwalk for some New American fare that's either wood-fired, farm-to-table, or both.

Kick off day two by visiting the Unitarian Church in Westport, a 25-minute drive northeast of Stamford. The church was designed by Victor A. Lundy and completed in 1965. The design was inspired by two praying hands, between which a shard of light filters into the minimalist interior. From there, drive 40 minutes northeast to New Haven to peruse the Yale University Art Gallery. The building, designed by Louis Kahn, is as impressive as the collection it houses and stands out magnificently among the neo-Gothic structures that surround it. Other must-sees in New Haven include Breuer's brutalist Pirelli Tire Building and the even more brutal Johansen-designed

Congregational United Church of Christ. And make sure not to forget Yale's Ingalls Rink, designed by Eero Saarinen and more fittingly known as the "The Whale." Finally, get a room at The Study and book a table at Heirloom, both located in a modern hotel on Yale campus.

New Canaan is home to the iconic Johnson's Glass House.

On the final day, it's on to Hartford, the state capital and home of the Wadsworth Atheneum Museum of Art. Particularly interesting is the associated Austin House, whose

walls have welcomed the likes of Salvador Dalí, Alexander Calder, and Gertrude Stein, as well as the relentless modernist Le Corbusier. One look inside and you'll see why. From there, it's just a short drive to the Mark Twain House & Museum, which is absolutely not modern but nevertheless a must-visit for its utmost encapsulation of American High Gothic. Finally, wrap up your whirlwind of a tour at the "Boat Building," which is famous for being the world's first two-sided tower. If nothing else, it's at least timeless—isn't that all you can ask of architecture? ◆

Bicycle America's Renowned Route to Freedom along the Underground Railroad

MOBILE, ALABAMA → OWEN SOUND, ONTARIO, CANADA

The treacherous passage used to escape slavery
in the South stands today as a testament to the bravery
and ingenuity of freedom seekers and their allies.

Contrary to its name, the Underground Railroad was not a train chugging beneath the soil. It was actually a secret network of routes and safe houses offering food, shelter, and aid to enslaved African Americans fleeing the South to free states in the North and countries like Canada and Mexico. Since the Fugitive Slave Act of 1850 allowed enslavers to recapture runaways, true liberation often meant leaving the United States entirely.

Though the exact operational dates of the Underground Railroad are unknown, it's thought to have existed from the late 18th century to the Civil War. At its height of operation, the Railroad provided escape for nearly 1,000 enslaved people a year.

The Ohio River was once the border between slave states and free states.

The Adventure Cycling Association created the Underground Railroad Bicycle Route (UGRR) to memorialize the Railroad. This 2,000-mile (3,219-kilometer), 42-day bike trip stretches from Mobile, Alabama, to Owen Sound, Ontario, on an eight-state historical expedition.

Through Alabama, Mississippi, Tennessee, Kentucky, and Indiana, the corridor follows rivers and waterways, then beelines to border towns in Ohio, Pennsylvania, and New York before entering Canada. There, it hugs the shoreline of Lake Ontario all the way to Owen Sound.

Thousands of cyclists ride the UGRR annually, usually from early spring in the South (before the sweltering heat sets in) to September (before temperatures drop in the North). If you choose to skip the bike and travel via car, not only does your travel season widen, but you can also shorten the trip's duration to two weeks.

Start in Alabama's oldest city: Mobile. During the 1800s, it was a major port for delivering enslaved Africans to the United States. Today, the African American Heritage Trail showcases 40 sites that depict Mobile's complicated history.

Then go north where the Tensaw and Alabama rivers guide you past town squares, Confederate memorials, and historical plaques detailing American Indian battles. Camp or hike

Home to more than 250 bird species, the Blackwater National Wildlife Refuge is a waterfowl watcher's paradise. The nearby Harriet Tubman Memorial Garden commemorates the iconic abolitionist and political activist who escaped slavery and whose missions to free other enslaved people formed the backbone of the Underground Railroad.

at the Historic Blakeley State Park, a destination rich with history and notable as being the site of the last battle of the Civil War.

In Fulton, Mississippi, see the town's homage to the Underground Railroad: a 6-foot- (1.8-meter-) high marker built with old railroad ties. Lanterns flanking both sides hang at the same height as a person carrying the lights to illuminate the darkness. The marker also explains the significance of "Follow the Drinking Gourd," a folk song used by freedom seekers to encode escape instructions, and highlights Harriet Tubman, the woman famous for helping enslaved people on the Underground Railroad.

North of Fulton, connect with the Natchez Trace Parkway, a 444-mile (715-kilometer) recreational route maintained by the National Park

Service. The terrain gets hillier here, especially as you head through Tennessee (where you can dive into Civil War history at Shiloh National Military Park and Fort Donelson National Battlefield) and into Kentucky. Here, enjoy the forested scenery at Land Between the Lakes. The 6,800 acres (2,752 hectares) encompass one of the first national wildlife refuges, a region of leafy upland ridges and beaver marshes teeming with animals. Set up camp for the night and keep an eye out for roaming bison.

The Ohio River was once the border between slave states and free states. Ride beside its easy flow as you make your way through the Kentucky, Indiana, and Ohio countryside. The landscape wows with big climbs and steep descents, as well as plenty of Underground →

HISTORIC
UNDERGROUND RAILROAD
IN THE MID 1800'S, WATERWAYS
SUCH AS THE NYACK BROOK, WHICH
FLOWS HERE, SERVED AS IMPORTANT
LAND-MARKS FOR AFRICAN AMERICAN
SLAVES ESCAPING NORTH ALONG
THE 'UNDERGROUND RAILROAD'

JOSEPH MITLOF FAMILY
'LEST WE FORGET'

Markers in and around Nyack, New York, highlight key stops along the Underground Railroad between Brooklyn and Buffalo. It is estimated that, at its peak, nearly 1,000 enslaved people per year used the route to escape from slave-holding states.

→ Railroad sightseeing points. In Madison, Indiana, see the African Methodist Episcopal Church, whose members were heavily involved in the Railroad. And because African Americans were not allowed to attend Madison public schools, the church doubled as a schoolhouse, holding classes for children in the basement.

After you cross the river to Ohio, spend time in Ripley to explore the National Historic District, which shares the inspiring stories of locals who were integral to the Railroad. There was former enslaved person John Parker, for one. He purchased his freedom, the act known as manumission, and went on to help enslaved people traverse the passage from Kentucky to Ohio. And there was Presbyterian minister John Rankin, who provided shelter to nearly 2,000 enslaved people, all of whom found the Rankin home by its single candle glowing in a window.

Keep driving on to Cincinnati and visit the city's 16-mile (26-kilometer) spur of the Underground Railroad. Don't miss the National Underground Railroad Freedom Center, the most comprehensive facility in the United States detailing the stories—both heroic and tragic—of the Railroad.

For lodging in Cincinnati, book a room at Six Acres. Not only are the accommodations well appointed, but the bed-and-breakfast holds an important place in Underground Railroad history. It was built by Quaker abolitionist Zebulon Strong. He transported freedom seekers in the false bottom of his farm wagon to his home (now Six Acres) for a good night's sleep before shuttling them to the next safe house.

The next leg of the UGRR includes 50 miles (80 kilometers) of the Little Miami Scenic Trail. This paved rail trail is one of the longest of its kind in the country, and it connects to the 272-mile (438-kilometer), off-street, perfect-for-bike-touring Ohio to Erie Trail. Hop on it in Milford, Ohio, and wind through a bucolic setting of sweeping farmlands, sun-dappled forests, and rushing rivers to Xenia.

From there, take a worthy detour to Springboro, Ohio, accessible via the UGRR spur from Waynesville. Springboro was founded by Quaker Jonathan Wright, whose anti-slavery stance evolved the town into one of the most popular stops on the Underground Railroad. →

Many settlements along Lake Erie served as points of entry to Canada for enslaved persons fleeing the United States. In Ontario, too, markers commemorate the Underground Railroad and all those who sought freedom from slavery.

→ The Springboro Area Historical Society estimates 4,000 people found a path to freedom through Springboro, and the society has documented nearly 30 safe houses. Spend the night in one of these—the cozy Wright House, Jonathan Wright's former home turned bed-and-breakfast.

Travel northeast through Columbus, pass through Mt. Vernon and Millersburg, and stop in Akron to see the home of abolitionist John Brown. He incited the enslaved peoples rebellion of Harpers Ferry, an event that eventually led to his execution.

The passage through Ohio's Ashtabula County shepherds you over covered bridges and through scenic wine country. It also takes you by dozens of Underground Railroad safe houses. To visit these, pedal the 44-mile (71-kilometer) Western Reserve Greenway, 27 miles (43 kilometers) of which are in Ashtabula County. Interpretive markers punctuate the route, identifying safe houses like Hubbard House. Listed on the National Register of Historic Places, Hubbard is now a museum commemorating the area's proud role in the Railroad.

More safe houses key to the cause are found around Buffalo, New York. Because of its proximity to Canada—a final destination for many enslaved people—and the anti-slavery sentiment in this part of the United States, this region offered numerous spots for safe harbor. One such place: the Michigan Street Baptist Church. Built in 1845, the church was a meeting spot for abolitionists, and it provided sanctuary to hundreds of enslaved people before they crossed the border. Central figures in Black history, such as Frederick Douglass, W. E. B. Du Bois, and Booker T. Washington, have all stepped through its doors.

From Buffalo, the UGRR utilizes the Niagra River Recreation Trail to enter Canada. Before you leave New York, though, take a 31-mile (50-kilometer) spur north to Murphy Orchards. The owners of the 1850 homestead, now a National Park Service partner open for tours, served as Railroad "station masters" who hid freedom seekers beneath their barn.

Once in Canada, you will see plaques along the trail honoring people and places of the Underground Railroad, from Ontario's first Coloured Corps to Harriet Tubman, who lived in the area for a decade. Then you'll arrive at Owen

Sound, the final terminal of the Underground Railroad. If you time your trip right, you can join the town's Emancipation Celebration held every August since 1862. It celebrates the British Emancipation Act of 1834 and the United States Emancipation Proclamation of 1863.

Owen Sound marks the trail's conclusion. For runaway enslaved people, this final stop of the Underground Railroad signaled the end of a long journey fraught with danger, reliant on the help of strangers, and clouded by the unknown. But it was also one filled with hope for that very thing owed to every human: freedom. ◆

DISTANCE
approx. 2,000 mi
(3,219 km)

DURATION
42 days by bike/
2 weeks by
motorized vehicle

BEST SEASON
Spring, Fall

CANADA

OWEN SOUND

LAKE ONTARIO

Michigan

★ Murphy Orchards
● Buffalo

New York

USA

Illinois

Indiana

Akron

Mount Vernon
Millersburg

Columbus
Xenia

Ohio

Springboro
Milford

Madison

Underground
Railroad
Freedom Center
in Cincinnati

West
Virginia

Pennsylvania

Virginia

Kentucky

★ Fort Donelson
National Battlefield

*Shiloh National
Military Park*

Tennessee

North
Carolina

South
Carolina

ROUTE
TRACING SLAVE
HISTORY

Alabama

Georgia

Mississippi

● Fulton

*Historic Blakeley
State Park*

MOBILE

41 MI (66 KM)

Hop from Island to Island among Georgia's Golden Isles

SAVANNAH, GEORGIA →
CUMBERLAND ISLAND, GEORGIA

Where Georgia meets the Atlantic, colonial history and crashing coastlines are just a causeway away.

If you don't know what a causeway is, you're about to get familiar. These raised roads are your connection to the Golden Isles, carrying you over coastal wetlands to some of the Atlantic shore's most majestic—and historic—spots. Covering about 170 miles (274 kilometers), this road trip takes around half a week to finish. But with so much to see and do, why not plan a little longer? Try to go in September or October when the crowds have died down but the water's still warm enough for a dip.

Bring a box of chocolates to Chippewa—there's a reason locals know it better as Forrest Gump Square.

Georgia has 14 major barrier islands, four of which belong to the Golden Isles: St. Simons Island, Sea Island, Jekyll Island, and Little St. Simons Island. The islands draw millions of visitors year-round thanks to balmy temperatures during the winter months.

Savannah serves as the gateway to your Georgia islands tour. Here, in the state's oldest settlement, you'll get a glimpse of how things used to be: people-first urban planning, antebellum architecture, and that unmistakable Southern hospitality. Spend a day walking under the ancient oaks and through the city's signature squares, none more famous than Chippewa. Bring a box of chocolates—there's a reason locals know it better as Forrest Gump Square. Ask around where you can find the best shrimp and grits and consider booking a night at the historic Kehoe House. The next morning, it's off to Tybee Island.

A stone's throw from Savannah, the beach at Tybee Island is the liveliest spot on the coast. There you'll find no shortage of seafood joints and other assorted lunch options, though you'd be remiss not to stop in at Wiley's Championship BBQ en route to the dunes. Post beach day, move on to the town of Darien. Spend the night there and mill about the next morning until you've worked up an appetite for Skippers' Fish Camp. After lunch, take a ferry to Sapelo Island, far removed from the crowds of yesterday. Marvel at the unspoiled splendor of Blackbeard Island National Wildlife Refuge or savor the seclusion of Nanny Goat Beach before making your way back to the mainland.

Next stop: Jekyll Island. On the way, take a slight detour to St. Simons for a history lesson at Fort Frederica National Monument. Then learn a little more at the World War II Home Front Museum. Finally, reward yourself with oysters at Dorothy's. Once on Jekyll, find a cozy spot to park your ride because this island's best seen on two wheels. More than 20 miles (32 kilometers) of paved paths are ready to be explored by bike, leading you through forests, marshes, beaches, and plenty of places to pull over for a bite to eat. There's always something to discover on the shores of Driftwood Beach, likewise at the nearby Horton Pond with its plethora of wildlife. (Pro tip: watch for gators.) As for the island's regal aura, that's left over from the Jekyll Island Club era when, starting in 1886, some of America's most storied families—Rockefellers, Morgans, Vanderbilts, Pulitzers, et al.—used Jekyll as their personal →

Some of America's most storied families used Jekyll Island as their personal playground. The "who's who" of the elite can still be spotted at the Jekyll Island Club Resort.

Save some days to explore Savannah and its ancient oaks, some of which are older than the city itself. You'll immediately notice Savannah's unique urban layout, highlighted by green public squares and residential wards.

→ playground. The "who's who" of the elite can still be spotted at the Jekyll Island Club Resort.

A little further down the coast lies the charming little town of St. Mary's. Spending a night at the Goodbread House or Spencer House Inn will give you an idea of the vibe of the place, or at least how it used to be. Make sure to track down Bessie's On The Move, a beloved local food truck serving up classics like cheesesteak and Buffalo fried chicken sandwiches.

From St. Mary's you have easy access (ferry only) to Cumberland Island and its pristine beaches. Most of the action happens on the south side. Check out the Dungeness ruins that straddle the Saltwater Marsh Boardwalk. A little further up, you'll find the Sea Camp Campground, which is as close to sleeping in nature as it gets. Bring bug spray—and something to swim in. The nearby beach is marvelous, as are the hiking options. Those with more experience may be tempted to set off for the lighthouse at the northern tip of the island.

At Tybee Island you'll find no shortage of seafood joints.

Frolicking the high dunes and shallow waters that surround it will be well worth the effort to get there. Just don't forget to save some energy for the return. If open-sky sleepovers and multiday walks are outside of your comfort zone, you'll find cozier quarters at the magnificent Greyfield Inn. No matter how you do it, one thing's for sure: the longer you jaunt around the Golden Isles, the harder it'll be to get back to landlocked living. ◆

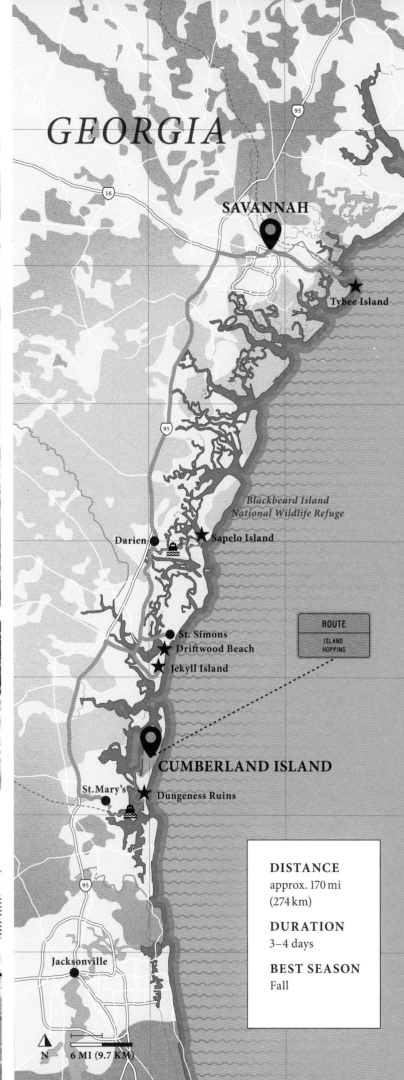

GEORGIA

95

16

SAVANNAH

Tybee Island

95

Blackbeard Island
National Wildlife Refuge

Darien

Sapelo Island

St. Simons
Driftwood Beach

Jekyll Island

ROUTE

ISLAND
HOPPING

CUMBERLAND ISLAND

St. Mary's

Dungeness Ruins

95

Jacksonville

DISTANCE
approx. 170 mi
(274 km)

DURATION
3–4 days

BEST SEASON
Fall

N   6 MI (9.7 KM)

Dive Into the Hospitality and Diversity of the Deep South

AUSTIN, TEXAS → CHARLESTON, SOUTH CAROLINA

The Southern states are often lumped together, but in one trip, you can witness the variety below the surface.

No trip to the Deep South would be complete without a stop in the Big Easy. Indulge in New Orleans's round-the-clock nightlife and vibrant live music scenes, and ask around for where to find the city's best gumbo, jambalaya, and boudin.

If you assume the Deep South to be a cultural monolith, then an adventure through some of its bigger cities and to some lesser-known diversions will change your mind. This trip celebrates the diversity you'll find along the Gulf Coast from Austin, Texas, through Louisiana, Mississippi, Alabama, and Georgia before arriving in Charleston, South Carolina.

Austin has courted a young, hip population over the last couple of decades and is now quite the creative hub. Sculptors Charles and Angeline Umlauf were part of the original wave of artists, and in 1985, they donated some 170 works to the city. You can find these works in the delightful Umlauf Sculpture Garden, a whimsical oasis to fire up your imagination as you begin your southern odyssey.

The Texan landscape is often thought of as boring and repetitive, but natural beauty is there if you know where to look. Take a break from the road with a dip in a magical grotto that boasts a 50-foot (15-meter) waterfall at Hamilton Pool Preserve, or just beyond that, the calm waters of the artesian spring at Jacob's Well.

Desert slowly transforms into swampland.

Joining I-10, the road that will guide you for the next few days. Eastern Texas can seem endless, but there's excitement to be found as

Houston comes into view. Space Center Houston is a Smithsonian-affiliated museum that celebrates the region's proud history of space travel. From moon rocks to vintage space suits and lunar modules, the exhibits here are a treasure trove of rare artifacts and a connection to those star-filled skies you'll see as night falls along those Texan country roads.

Desert slowly transforms into swampland as Louisiana approaches, the Gulf of Mexico making inroads into the coastline as you pass first Beaumont and then Lake Charles. Sometimes the swamp is visible from the highway, intriguing enough to warrant further exploration. A rickety shack at Lake Martin is the base for Champagne's Swamp Tours, where seasoned professionals can guide you through →

Don't let the term "swamplands" deter you—there's plenty of beauty to be found in the water-bogged regions of the Deep South. Take a riverboat cruise, go kayaking, and get your fill of crawfish. Just keep an eye out for gators.

→ the centuries-old cypress forests, spotting birdlife and gators along the way.

Most visitors to New Orleans come for the music and the food, but a history of piracy gives the city's lore some color. The most infamous of the pirates is Jean Lafitte, and most walking tours will educate you on how this local legend helped the Americans repel the British at the Battle of New Orleans. Such was his popularity that you can also explore the nearby nature of Jean Lafitte National Historical Park and Preserve, where pirates once hid away from prying eyes and meddling authority.

You should, of course, make time for the food here. Gumbo, jambalaya, and boudin are available year-round, and if you're here in the right season (usually January–June), then a communal crawfish boil is as Louisianan as it gets. New Orleans is also famous for its annual Mardi Gras celebrations, of course, although nearby Mobile has some claims on being the regional originators of this celebratory tradition.

Natural beauty is there if you know where to look.

Locals in this Alabama city will argue that it was here, not in New Orleans, that Mardi Gras in America was born, some 300 years ago. The Mobile Carnival Museum makes a strong case, citing the first observation of the feast by Frenchman Nicholas Langlois in 1703. The museum has a wealth of exhibits showing the evolution of the local event, including the gowns and jewels that were worn by Carnival Queens throughout the years.

The recent history of the South is impossible to tell without paying attention to the Civil Rights Movement. The Civil Rights District in Birmingham, Alabama, is a kind of living museum encompassing several important historic sites that interpret the city's role in the movement. Self-guided tours take visitors past landmarks such as the 16th Street Baptist Church, which was bombed by white supremacists in 1963. Multimedia exhibits illustrate civil rights struggles as well as inroads into future harmony including the Civil Rights Act of 1964. →

Bayou life has a certain irresistible pull. So much so, in fact, that Creedence Clearwater Revival's John Fogerty wrote "Born on the Bayou" despite being from California and never before having visited Louisiana.

→ You can also pay your respects to beloved civil rights leaders at the Martin Luther King, Jr. National Historical Park as you arrive in Atlanta. This urban National Historic Landmark includes Dr. King's birth home and several memorials including a statue of Mahatma Gandhi, who was a constant inspiration. The International Civil Rights Walk of Fame pays homage to many others who fought so bravely for equality.

Stark realities are important to acknowledge, but escapism provides a welcome balance. After Atlanta's concrete sprawl, you'll appreciate the moss-laden city squares and genteel architecture of Savannah, Georgia. This is a city that has cultivated a cultured, urbane reputation that is underpinned by mystery and intrigue, not to mention the supernatural.

These disparate elements are woven together in its most famous literary work, Midnight in the Garden of Good and Evil, a 1994 "nonfiction novel" by the author John Berendt.

The Deep South is anything but shallow.

High society, true crime, and voodoo meet over the course of the novel, and the garden of the title plays a central role. This is a real place, a rural graveyard just east of the city center called Bonaventure Cemetery. The many tree-lined pathways and striking angel sculptures

provide a suitably evocative and (as the sun sets) spooky ambiance.

After swimming holes, space travel, swamps, pirates, carnivals, civil rights, and ghost stories, the final stop is the relatively buttoned-down city of Charleston, South Carolina. World-class historic architecture is the last feature of this esoteric road trip. This city dates back to the late 17th century and boasts almost 3,000 historic buildings. There's a visible progression through the ages as political, social, and aesthetic movements took place, resulting in a spectrum of styles: Colonial, Georgian, Federal, Classical Revival, Gothic Revival, Italianate, Victorian, and Art Deco. Take a guided walking tour or visit a specific property, and the city's stories will tell themselves through the masonry.

This region is subject to many precon-
ceptions, and a trip that passes through such
different geographic and social landscapes is a
great way to dispel them. There's as much variety
here as you'll find in any region but with some
delightful consistencies along the way. The food,
from Texan barbecue to Cajun delicacies to the
fresh seafood of the Gulf Coast, is irresistible,
and the sense of hospitality you should encounter
along the way is world famous for a reason.
Open yourself up and indulge your curious side,
and you'll find that the Deep South is anything
but shallow. ◆

DISTANCE
approx. 1,755 mi
(2,824 km)

DURATION
10 days

BEST SEASON
Spring, Winter

Arkansas

USA

Oklahoma
City

Texas

Dallas

Louisiana

Hamilton Pool
Preserve

Jacob's Well

AUSTIN

Lake Charles

Lake Martin

Beaumont

Houston

Space Center Houston

San Antonio

MEXICO

N
28 MI (45 KM)

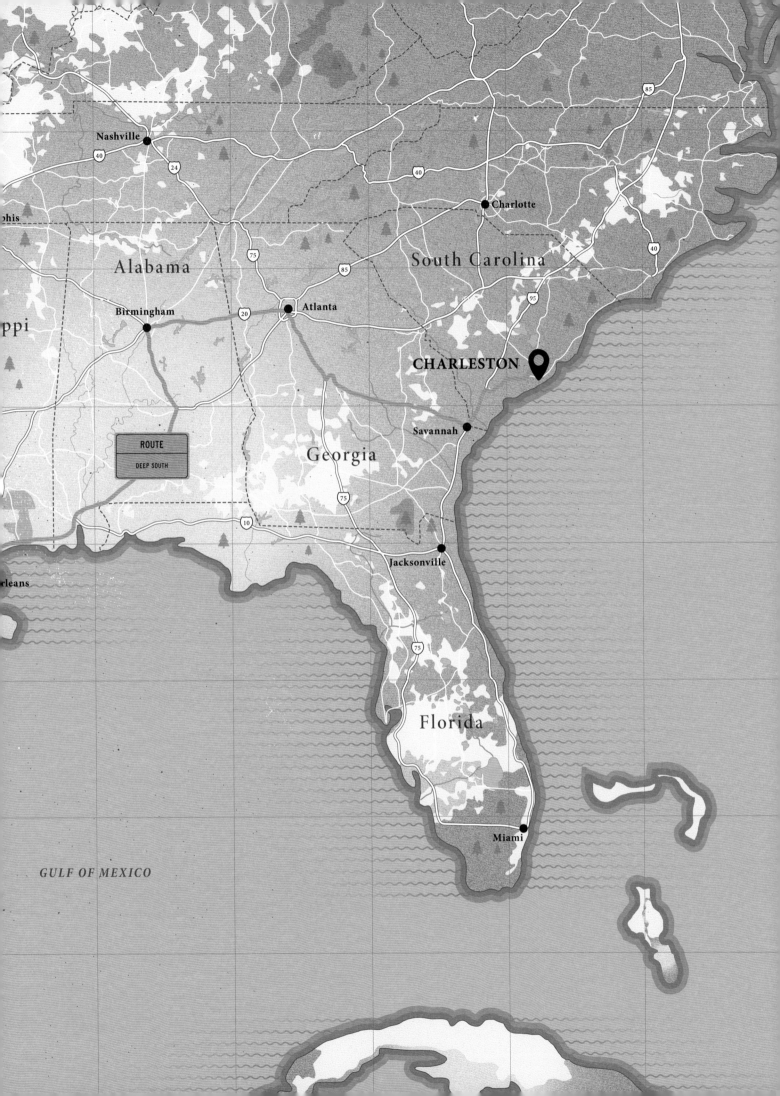

Follow the Sound
of the South, Combined
in Perfect Harmony

NASHVILLE, TENNESSEE → NEW ORLEANS, LOUISIANA

Three cities in the Deep South have equally rich but varied
musical histories, and you can tune into them.

Catch the blues every night of the week at dozens of venues on Memphis's Beale Street. While the blues originated from work and folk songs as early as the 1860s, artists like Frank Stokes, Sleepy John Estes, Furry Lewis, and Memphis Minnie put a local spin on the genre from the 1910s to the 1930s.

Country, jazz, and blues can all claim to be truly American art forms, and on a 600-mile (966-kilometer) stretch of road through the Deep South, you can experience their roots. You'll also find places that gave rise to myths and legends—the crossroads where Robert Johnson was said to have dealt with the devil, or the streets where Louis Armstrong sang for change as a child. This drive is drenched in cultural history, a celebration of live music in all of its forms, and as a delicious bonus, you'll find some of the country's most enticing food.

Nashville has the nickname "Music City" and for good reason. If you get tickets to a show at a historic venue such as The Grand Ole Opry, you can almost feel the legacy of generations of musicians ring out. Whether or not you go as far

as to don a Stetson and bolo tie (sold at any of the outfitters on Broadway), you can commune with the spirits of the legends.

You'll find places that gave rise to myths and legends.

Just take a walk along the infamous Ryman Alley, from the gates of the Ryman Auditorium to the back door of Tootsie's Orchid Lounge. Guitars sing from almost every bar downtown, cowboys and country queens letting it rip in spit-and-sawdust honky-tonk joints as they have for decades.

Fuel up on some spicy goodness at Prince's Hot Chicken Shack before the easy three-hour drive to Memphis, a straight shot west along I-40. The suburbs may recede, but the musical history along this stretch remains vibrant. Johnny Cash and June Carter sang about Jackson in the famously prickly song of the same name, and in Brownsville, a young woman named Anna Mae Bullock began her career singing in the church choir. There's now a museum dedicated to her under her stage name: Tina Turner.

As you approach Memphis, the sultry allure of the Mississippi Delta begins to take hold, the hearty twang of country morphing into the stoic slide of the blues. You'll likely be drawn to the neon lights of Beale Street, and while →

Ground Zero Blues Club, co-owned by the actor Morgan Freeman, is a local favorite in Clarksdale. More grunge than glam, the juke joint lends its stage to local musicians and well-known performers alike.

→ you can find authenticity in these slick venues, the real blues thrives in less salubrious surroundings. Historically, blues musicians would strike up without too much in the way of ceremony at "juke joints," and while most have disappeared, Wild Bill's is a modern approximation. Grab a 40-ounce (1.2-liter) beer, sit at a table with strangers, and soak in the music.

In Memphis, you can reach out and touch musical history. You can find yourself standing in the recording booth at Sun Studios, your feet where the Million Dollar Quartet once stood: Elvis Presley, Jerry Lee Lewis, Carl Perkins, and Johnny Cash. Or you can sit in the pew of a Mississippi Delta church at the Stax Museum of American Soul Music. The twinkle from Isaac Hayes's glittering custom Cadillac Eldorado will

definitely catch your eye as you move through the exhibits.

If there are pilgrims in Memphis, though, they're most likely here to pay their respects to Elvis Presley.

Sit at a table with strangers and soak in the music.

The decadence of his former home, Graceland, seems picturesque by modern standards, but fans find solace in seeing the famous Jungle Room, sitting in The King's private jet, and having their own moment of

musical transcendence standing at Presley's final resting place.

Many came before Elvis, though, and you'll find the deep musical roots of this region in towns like Clarksdale, Mississippi, an hour's drive south along US-61. This road alone has significance, with artists like Bob Dylan paying homage to the highway that connected his hometown of Duluth to the Mississippi Delta on his album Highway 61 Revisited. Dylan said of the highway that it was "full of the same contradictions, the same one-horse towns, the same spiritual ancestors."

If there's an ancestral home in these parts, it's definitely Clarksdale. The state-endorsed Mississippi Blues Trail emanates from here. A patchwork of historical markers that helps →

Rock 'n' roll owes as much to blues pioneers like Muddy Waters as it does to its own early stars of the genre. All across the state, you'll find odes to local musicians and the impact they've had on shaping music not only in America but around the world.

→ visitors interpret their surroundings in relation to the musicians that came up along the way. You can start your education listening to the stripped-down sets at the bare bones of the Ground Zero Blues Club, suitably named as one of the epicenters of the blues. It's hard not to tap into the emotion as the musicians on stage strike up a plaintive chord.

The history is so rich here that myths have been created. The most famous is that of Robert Johnson, perhaps the most respected blues practitioner of all time, sold his soul to the devil for his incredible guitar skills at the intersection of Highway 61 and Highway 49. Bluesmen of his caliber have stayed at the still-operational Riverside Hotel since the mid-1940s, and memorabilia from even earlier days

can be seen at the Delta Blues Museum, where former belongings of Muddy Waters and Big Mama Thornton are revered as holy relics.

US-61 meanders down along the curves of the Mississippi Delta, following the flow of the mighty river.

You'll hear jazz flooding out from every venue.

Across the flat swamplands, the Crescent City of New Orleans slowly comes into view. Hundred-year-old architecture gives way to 300-year-old buildings, replete with iron balconies of Spanish

colonialism, French and Caribbean influences also making themselves known.

Cocktails—a Sazerac, maybe, or a Ramos Gin Fizz—are almost obligatory as you stroll through the cinematic streets of the historic French Quarter. Bourbon Street has less live jazz now and more karaoke bars, but duck into the cellar at Fritzel's and the rock music gives way to brass and woodwind. Just around the corner, you can line up for tickets to the dusty showroom at Preservation Hall, where traditional "Dixieland" jazz rules the roost, and where crowds are applauding multiple shows per night. Take a short walk to Frenchmen Street, and you'll hear jazz flooding out from almost every venue, cozy clubs such as The Blue Nile and The Spotted Cat packed with revelers and swing dancers.

Country music, the blues, and jazz all have their histories and their heroes. It's a testament to the culture of the Deep South that these traditions are celebrated and conserved, not just in the old venues but in each of the generations that comes through playing live music, paying homage to those that came before. You can pay your own respects, find the music that speaks to you, and as you drive, put on some tunes and appreciate the birthplaces of some of America's most beloved cultural and musical traditions. ◆

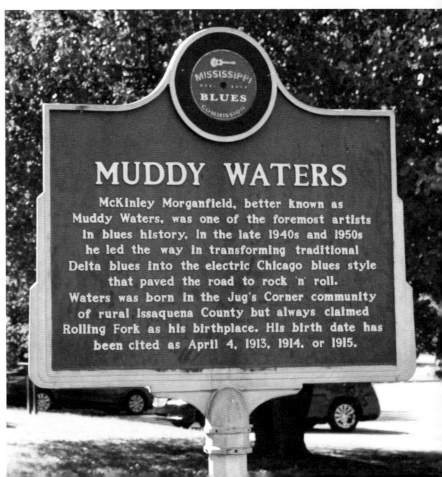

MUDDY WATERS

McKinley Morganfield, better known as Muddy Waters, was one of the foremost artists in blues history. In the late 1940s and 1950s he led the way in transforming traditional Delta blues into the electric Chicago blues style that paved the road to rock 'n' roll.
Waters was born in the Jug's Corner community of rural Issaquena County but always claimed Rolling Fork as his birthplace. His birth date has been cited as April 4, 1913, 1914, or 1915.

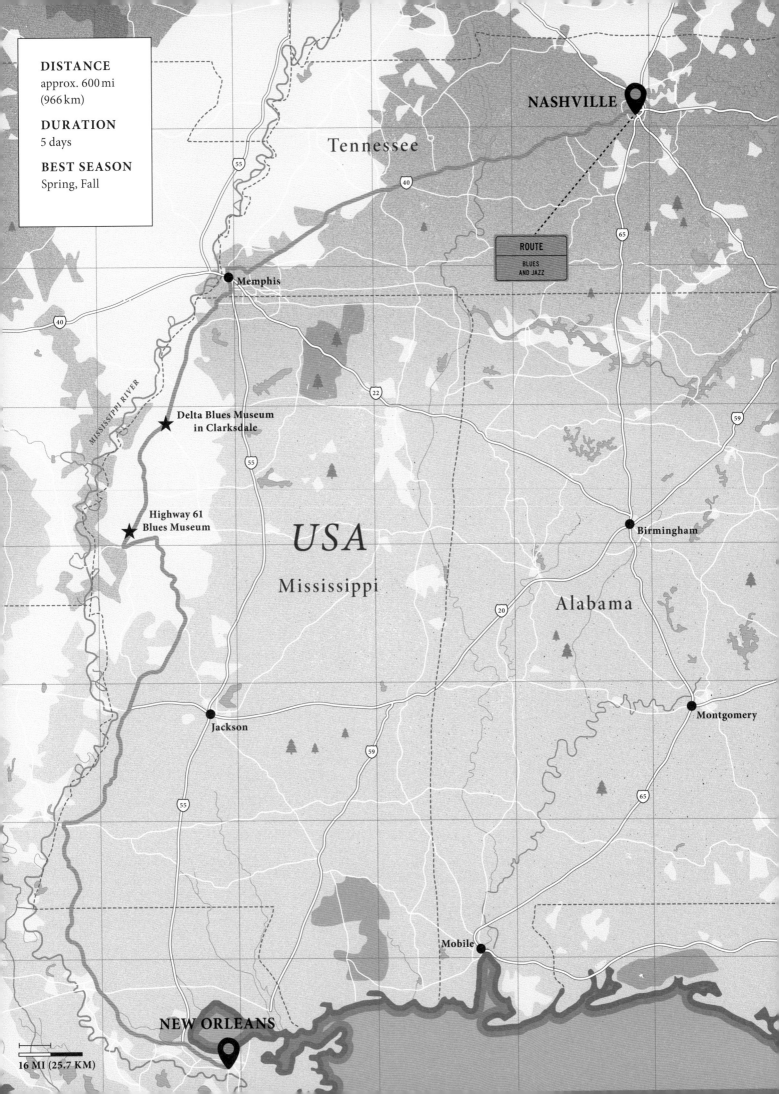

DISTANCE
approx. 600 mi
(966 km)

DURATION
5 days

BEST SEASON
Spring, Fall

ROUTE

BLUES
AND JAZZ

NASHVILLE

Tennessee

55

40

● Memphis

40

MISSISSIPPI RIVER

★ Delta Blues Museum
in Clarksdale

55

22

★ Highway 61
Blues Museum

USA

Mississippi

65

59

● Birmingham

Alabama

20

● Jackson

55

59

● Montgomery

65

● Mobile

NEW ORLEANS

16 MI (25.7 KM)

Taste the Big Smoke:
A Journey through the
Barbecue Belt of Texas

AUSTIN, TEXAS → SAN ANTONIO, TEXAS

The art of smoking is a serious business in Texas, and
you can sample the best on this meat-heavy journey.

If Texas can be said to have an equivalent of an indigenous cuisine, then it has to be barbecue. In its purest form, it's a culinary technique that dates back millennia. The basic theory is simply meat cooked over an open flame, a process that is as unpretentious and common sense as the state itself. Yet, where an activity enjoys such ubiquitous popularity and is taken so seriously, it follows that nuance, experimentation, and commitment to the highest levels of quality. For fans of smoked meat, put simply, this is a highway to heaven.

On this carnivorous pilgrimage, you may find competing—and in some cases, even vehemently opposing—views on what constitutes "real" barbecue. You'll also find reassuring constants in the accompaniments to all of these experiences, though. Cold beer, live music, and a sincere welcome should be the essential ingredients that make for a memorable barbecue regardless of the approach; and Texas usually comes through on these basics. Bear in mind that you'd need a superhuman appetite to sample every suggested stop in this short pilgrimage, so take time to plan around whatever sounds most appealing.

Cold beer, live music, and a sincere welcome should be the essential ingredients that make for a memorable barbecue.

It's sometimes easy to forget that Austin is the Texan capital and not Dallas. With its "Bat City" nickname and the "Keep Austin Weird" sloganeering, it's a more bohemian and liberal place than you might figure for this part of the world. The barbecue scene here is ferociously competitive, a steady stream of influencers and young foodies keeping the scene on its toes. Ask ten locals for their favored spot and you'll likely receive ten different answers, with hushed tones reserved for the beef ribs at Iron Works or the pulled pork at Franklin Barbecue. Make your peace with standing in line; it's well worth the wait.

Drive an hour northeastward across the seemingly infinite flat, grassy plains of Southern Texas. An unassuming former railroad town

East Texas, Central Texas, South Texas, and West Texas aren't just geographical regions but also distinct styles of barbecue. Drive all across the state to taste-test the best of each genre, from beef brisket to pork ribs and sausage, plus all of the necessary sides.

awaits, with centuries of Germanic commitment to meat dishes at the end of the trail. In the late 19th century, this region welcomed waves of immigrants from Germany, Austria, and the Czech Republic, and these meat-loving peoples brought their expertise with them. The town of Taylor is your base, and your goals are the brisket at Buckalew's, the mesquite-sweetened ribs at Davis BBQ, and the all-beef sausages at Louie Mueller, at the top of their game since 1949.

Just 16 miles (26 kilometers) south on State Hwy 95 is Elgin, which boldly claims the title of the "Sausage Capital of Texas" amid a glut of rivalry. At Southside Market, a version of their famous hot sausage has been served to hungry locals for over 125 years. Four generations of the Meyer family have been making and

serving their pork garlic sausages at Meyer's Elgin Smokehouse for some 75 years. With traditions and honed smoking skills like these, that title is near impossible to wrestle away.

Closing the loop through Austin, this time exiting southwestward, and we're firmly in Texas Hill Country as we arrive in Driftwood, around 25 miles (40 kilometers) from the city. The historic buildings and small-town atmosphere give the place an air of a pioneering outpost, and that's what it likely was when the ancestors of Thurman Roberts arrived in 1867. Exactly 100 years later, Roberts and his wife Hisako built a huge open fire pit and opened The Salt Lick. That pit still operates today, and barbecue fans travel from far and wide to try the brisket and the special sweet barbecue sauce.

The countryside around Driftwood is the ideal place to walk off some of these meat-heavy meals. Charro Ranch Park opens up into 64 acres (26 hectares) of hiking and nature trails, with 120 species of bird calling it home for at least part of the year. Also among the gentle hills, several vineyards enjoy idyllic locations, with Fall Creek Vineyards, Duchman Family Winery, and the Driftwood Estate Winery among the best.

Staying in Hill Country, FM 150 snakes southeastward towards Lockhart, just an hour or so away. There may be some passionate discussion on the subject, but since 2003, Lockhart has enjoyed the official state title of "The Barbecue Capital of Texas." There are four barbecue restaurants, and a quarter of a million people come to sample their fares every year. →

Drive an hour northeastward across the seemingly infinite flat, grassy plains of Southern Texas. An unassuming former railroad town awaits, with centuries of Germanic commitment to meat dishes at the end of the trail.

Barbecue traditions in Texas are as old as the state itself. Today, they're being kept alive by a promising generation of newcomers who stay anchored in tried-and-true methods that have become renowned the world over.

→ Black's is one of the oldest barbecue restaurants in the state and uses prime Angus beef for their world-famous brisket. Kreuz Market (pronounced "Krites") is a sauce-averse joint where beef, sausage, and pork are served on brown butcher paper. Chisholm Trail and Smitty's Market have both been satisfying guests for well over half a century. Lockhart State Park awaits exploration for visitors looking to shake off a few calories or wanting to switch up their menu by fishing for bass, catfish, or sunfish.

It's a straight shot down US-183 to Luling, just 20 minutes south. Look no further than the lively halls of Luling City Market, where the "holy trinity" of barbecue (sausage, brisket, and ribs) is bestowed on devout pilgrims. The

other game in town is watermelon, and Luling loves this fruit so much that they host an annual four-day festival, the Watermelon Thump.

The "holy trinity" of barbecue? Sausage, brisket, and ribs.

At any time, though, it's a delight to take a few sweet slices and eat them on the banks of the San Marcos River.

One more hour on the road, this time east, is the final stop of San Antonio. Work up an appetite seeing the city's famous historic spots, from the Alamo to the ancient missions and the

Riverwalk, and then submit once more to the barbecue. Newcomers are making waves here, with 2M Smokehouse and Pinkerton's BBQ, both nationally acclaimed since opening in 2016 and 2021, respectively. Head to old-school Mexican places for some cabrito, a roasted goat specialty.

Remove the barbecue blinders once in a while to try other regional delicacies, including Rocky Mountain Oysters (battered and fried bull testicles), aligot (cheesy mashed potatoes), and kolaches, a Czech pastry that is now a Texan classic. It's all fine fuel for the road, and the best thing about this trip is that there are plenty of places to fill up. ◆

The barbecue scene here is ferociously competitive, a steady stream of influencers and young foodies keeping the scene on its toes.

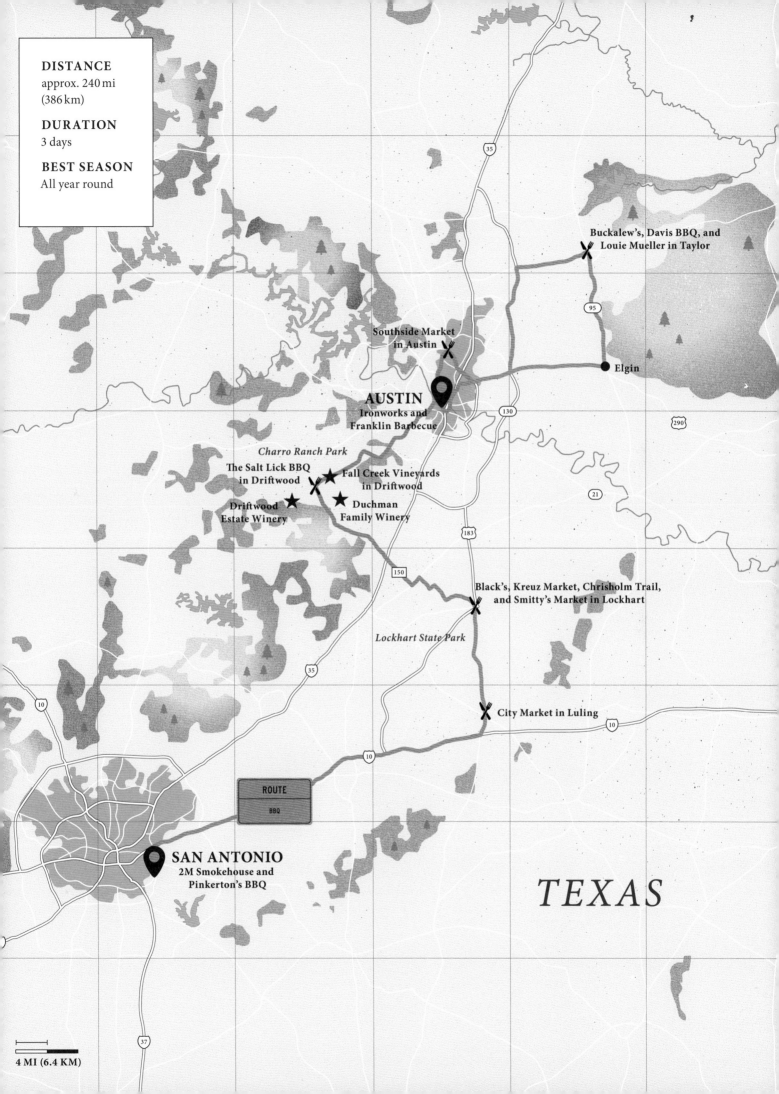

DISTANCE
approx. 240 mi
(386 km)

DURATION
3 days

BEST SEASON
All year round

Buckalew's, Davis BBQ, and
Louie Mueller in Taylor

⁹⁵

35

Southside Market
in Austin

Elgin

130

AUSTIN
Ironworks and
Franklin Barbecue

290

Charro Ranch Park

The Salt Lick BBQ
in Driftwood

Fall Creek Vineyards
in Driftwood

21

Driftwood
Estate Winery

Duchman
Family Winery

183

150

Black's, Kreuz Market, Chrisholm Trail,
and Smitty's Market in Lockhart

Lockhart State Park

35

City Market in Luling

10

10

ROUTE

BBQ

SAN ANTONIO
2M Smokehouse and
Pinkerton's BBQ

TEXAS

37

4 MI (6.4 KM)

Watch the Skies: Stargazing in the Lone Star State

HOUSTON, TEXAS → AMARILLO, TEXAS

The beauty of the star-filled desert
skies is complemented by modern art
in unlikely places.

Everything's bigger in Texas as the saying goes, and however you look at it, the Lone Star State is the second-largest in the United States both in area and population. This means huge cities, divided by vast tracts of wide-open countryside with nothing to be seen for miles and miles. You can drive for days and still not cross state lines.

Now, Texas doesn't have the most exciting scenery—there's no Grand Canyon or mountain ranges to break up the monotony. However, the endless stretches of rural landscape mean that if you cast your eyes skywards, you'll be rewarded with views of the Milky Way that are quite breathtaking. The state has several designated "astrotourism zones" and dark sky sanctuaries—places especially suited to stargazing.

From Houston, you'd ideally fire up your RV or camper van. This road trip works best if you can spend time outdoors in the dead of night, and you'll need to have a comfortable place to sleep that doesn't involve dashing to motels.

Texas doesn't have the most exciting scenery. But if you cast your eyes skywards, you'll be rewarded with magnificent views.

At the edge of Hermann Park you'll find the Houston Museum of Natural Science, which operates the George Observatory—newly renovated and open for cosmos-watching and educational talks. We're still a little close to the urban sprawl to see much without hi-tech assistance, but that's all about to change.

Around four hours' drive, out past Austin, the landscape opens up. The Enchanted Rock State Natural Area has huge, pink granite domes that have fascinated humankind for centuries. The Tonkawa Tribe thought that ghostly fires flickered on these ancient slopes, but now people come to view different lights. The park is a class-three (class one being the best) International Dark Sky Park and hosts regular "Rock Star Parties" where rangers are on hand to point out constellations and shooting stars.

Breaking east into Texas Hill Country, you can turn your attention to the subterranean. →

Despite being America's second-most-populous state, Texas is also the second largest. That means there's plenty of space to get away from the lights and look skyward, where the stars are bigger and brighter than anywhere else in the country.

→ The Caverns of Sonora are widely held to be among the most beautiful show caves on Earth. Descend into a world of twinkling, crystal-rock formations and otherworldly stalactites and stalagmites, climaxing in "The Butterfly," the only known example of an astonishing "double fishtail" helictite formation.

Make sure that you've adjusted your sleep schedule for nighttime adventures as you approach Big Bend Ranch National Park, one of only a handful of class-one International Dark Sky Parks in the United States. In fact, it holds the enviable title of having the least light pollution of any national park in the Lower 48, such are the clarity and scope of the night sky here.

Most of the roads around the park are treeless, making for a stark, minimalist landscape.

Only the nearby Chisos Mountains are really visible as far as terrain features go, and they provide a striking background to stargazing and photography.

You can drive for days and still not cross state lines.

The depths of the Milky Way and fields of shooting stars are often visible from almost anywhere in this dark, remote region.

As the name suggests, the park really is too big to see in one day, but there are options. The Ross Maxwell Scenic Drive is perhaps the

most popular way to experience the Chisos Basin that takes in the Chihuahuan Desert landscape and the banks of the Rio Grande. Striking geological formations such as Tuff Canyon or Sotol Vista stand out, and beloved places such as Santa Elena Overlook or Mule Ears Viewpoint are among the best spots to settle in for a night appreciating those incredible skies.

Luxuriate fully in the space, both around and above you, before the short drive to the remote artistic enclave of Marfa. This quirky town was founded in the 1880s as a simple water stop for travelers, eventually becoming a military base. In 1971, everything changed when minimalist Donald Judd moved there and set up an artists' community. The scene has expanded and thrives to this day, the town surrounded

by galleries, workshops, and installations such as the famous re-creation of a Prada store on the edges of town.

Strange phenomena can be witnessed here. Take US-90 to the Mitchell Flats and, if you're lucky, you'll see the Marfa Lights, mysterious glowing orbs that appear in the desert. No provable explanation has been provided for these strange shapes, but they're likely some kind of environmentally induced mirage.

Slightly further out in the Chihuahuan Desert, the McDonald Observatory keeps a watchful eye on the skies. It has been there since 1939, and when it was built, it housed the second-largest telescope in the world. Located in the high peaks of the Davis Mountains, the observatory enjoys some of the darkest and clearest →

If you're lucky, you'll see the Marfa Lights, mysterious glowing orbs that appear in the desert. Nobody knows where they come from.

Everyone knows Houston, Dallas, San Antonio, and Austin. They are all great cities in their own right, but rural Texas is where the magic happens. And not just in the sky. Keep an eye on the horizon and see if you can spot the Marfa Lights, which could be caused by anything, really, depending on who you ask.

→ skies in the region, helping it track stars from the far reaches of interstellar space.

Your trip could end here, but if you have the time, it's worth extending north and pushing on to the small town of Ransom Canyon. Members of the Jumano, Apache, and Comanche tribes camped here for centuries, and Spanish explorers are thought to have crossed the canyon as early as the 1540s. Now it's a small town of around 1,000 residents just outside Lubbock. Its most famous landmarks are the Steel House and the Rock House—both large architectural art installations created by artists Robert Bruno and Mark Lawson, respectively. The former is an industrial steel construction, the latter a more whimsical cottage inspired by none other than Gaudí.

You're still far enough from city lights to enjoy stargazing here, and local astronomy clubs regularly hold Public Star Parties. Local experts set up their telescopes and encourage everyone to look at the planets, star clusters, and galaxies that are all visible in the night skies.

Local astronomy clubs regularly hold Public Star Parties.

Modern art has been a parallel theme of this road trip since Marfa, and there's one last exhibit to see before the final stop in Amarillo. In 1974, an art collective (with the backing of a local

millionaire) set up a line of ten Cadillacs with their noses driven into the dirt. A comment on materialism and human folly, the installations became known as Cadillac Ranch, and although the cars have been stripped and plastered in graffiti, the site is as popular as ever. If you pass by here around nightfall, it's perhaps worth one more look at the skies before you return to the city lights. ◆

Oklahoma

USA
Texas

AMARILLO
Cadillac Ranch

Ransom Canyon

ROUTE
STARGAZING

Oklahoma
City

Dallas

Donald
ervatory

Enchanted Rock State
Natural Area

Caverns of Sonora

Austin

Marfa

HOUSTON

Big Bend Ranch
National Park

George Observatory

RIO GRANDE

San Antonio

MEXICO

GULF OF MEXICO

DISTANCE
approx. 879 mi
(1,415 km)

DURATION
1–2 weeks

BEST SEASON
Spring, Fall

25 MI (40 KM)

Tour Old Texas by Motorcycle on the Twisted Sisters

MEDINA, TEXAS

An iconic motorcycle route takes you through the ups, downs, and arounds of Hill Country.

If you're looking for the Lone Star State's biggest thrill on two wheels, you'll find it in the Twisted Sisters. This iconic motorcycle route is named after a triplet of ranch roads—FM 335, FM 336, and FM 337—that feature more than 200 turns between them. "FM," in this case, refers to "farm-to-market," which should give an indication of the area's ruralness. Technically, you can start the 170-mile (274-kilometer) loop from anywhere and go in either direction. Most people prefer to kick off from the town of Medina, just 60 miles (97 kilometers) northwest of San Antonio. Really, though, city life couldn't feel further away.

There's really only one way to do it right, and that's on two wheels. The Twisted Sisters are among America's most revered motorcycle routes and offer a glimpse of the Lone Star State that few are familiar with.

The Sisters rise and dip like a rollercoaster up its plateaus and down its valleys with plenty to see left and right.

This being Texas, picture arid plains populated by pumpjacks and drifting tumbleweeds—just kidding. This is Texas Hill Country, a rugged and at times lush expanse that often surprises visitors and locals alike. The Sisters rise and dip like a rollercoaster up its plateaus and down its valleys with plenty to see left and right. The 335 runs parallel to the Nueces River, which makes for some stunning views on the off chance that you can take your eyes off the asphalt. If you're going southbound, you'll eventually meet the 337, which feels akin to being in a washing machine; the first 15 miles (24 kilometers) throw more

than 60 loops your way, and it gets only marginally more chill after that. Finally, the 336 is where things get steep and secluded, with little in the way of civilization. The Garven Store, a legendary jerky shop that's about to turn 90, is worth the short detour (8 minutes on TX-41E). With a standout barbecue brisket and a couple of gas pumps on the premises, you'd be seriously remiss not to pull in and fuel up.

Along the way, absolutely make a stop at Devil's Sinkhole and get a bird's-eye view of hell. And no, you're not tripping à la Hunter S. Thompson—this really is bat country (the giant cavern is home to millions of them). See it under a starry sky for an especially eerie atmosphere. From Vanderpool on 337, a short jaunt north (5 miles/1.6 kilometers) on RM-187 brings you

to Lost Maples State Natural Area—another great spot to drop your kickstand for a few hours. This natural treasure is highlighted by the snaking Sabinal River, which winds through a canyon brimming with wildlife: tarantulas, snakes, exotic deer, even mountain lions. And, since it's right on the way, you might as well swing by the Lone Star Motorcycle Museum, a local shrine with more than 60 models on display. Wrap up your time in the wilderness with a tasting at the Lost Maples Winery on the Sabinal riverfront (there's a lodge on-site where you can sleep off the libations).

How long you spend on the Twisted Sisters is up to you. Some do it in under half a day, others book a bed somewhere along the way and make a weekend of it. If you opt for the latter, consider →

Along the way, absolutely make a stop at Devil's Sinkhole and get a bird's-eye view of hell.

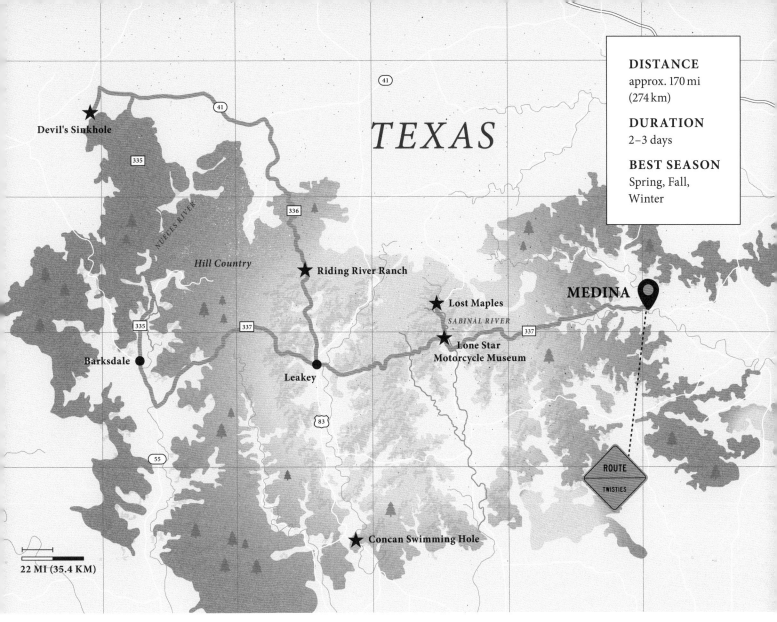

TEXAS

Devil's Sinkhole

Hill Country

NUECES RIVER

Riding River Ranch

Lost Maples

MEDINA

SABINAL RIVER

Lone Star
Motorcycle Museum

Barksdale

Leakey

Concan Swimming Hole

ROUTE

TWISTIES

22 MI (35.4 KM)

Swimming holes are a staple of Hill Country. Don't worry if you can't find a
private oasis like the one on offer at the Riding River Ranch. Seek a spot anywhere
along the West Frio River and plunge in after a long day on the hot asphalt.

→ staying at The Historic Leakey Inn, a charming lodge that looks like it lived through the Dust Bowl. Of course, no trip to Leakey would be complete without a bite at the impeccably named Bent Rim Grill. Cap it off with a dip at the Concan Swimming Hole in the majestic Frio River (20 minutes south on US-83) and you've pretty much lived Leakey to the fullest. For something a little more upscale, check in at the nearby Riding River Ranch, which comes with a private swimming hole and 3,400 acres (1,376 hectares) of land primed for hiking, off-roading, or just plain lazing around. Should it be fully booked, there's no shortage of camps and cabins further along the Frio River. Just meander your way along Old Rocksprings Road and you'll be bound to find someone who's happy to have you over.

It should be said that for all the joy of riding the Twisted Sisters, parts of the route can also test your talents. The twists are no joke, and there's a notable absence of guardrails on some sections.

City life couldn't feel further away.

You can differentiate between rookies and veterans of the road by how fast they're going. If it's your first time, err on the slower side. Another pro tip: avoid peak summer. Unless, of course, you're the cold-blooded type who can thrive in sweltering temperatures. Finally, don't forget to take in the Texas of it all: the fire-cooked fare, the rancher slang, the way the old hasn't yet met the new. There are few other places in America where you can so easily slip into the spirit of a bygone era—even while barreling through it on your motorbike. ◆

Glimpse Iconic Architecture and Impressive Art from Los Angeles to Marfa

LOS ANGELES, CALIFORNIA → MARFA, TEXAS

This trip ignites the creative spirit with inspiring works of art and renowned architectural marvels.

It's no secret that Los Angeles, with its fusion of diverse cultures, is a haven for creatives whose artistry shows up in murals, museums, and buildings. Los Angeles is an international hub after all. But what may come as a surprise is that places like middle-of-nowhere Marfa, Texas, or dusty Tucson, Arizona, are equally tempting locales for talented artists to paint, sculpt, design, and make stunning masterpieces waiting to be discovered.

On this 14-day, 1,300-mile (2,092-kilometer) trip, you'll get to do just that. Beginning in L. A., the art-themed trek travels east to the midcentury architecture of Palm Springs, then continues to the Arizona cities of Phoenix and Tucson before dipping south to New Mexico, and east to the art Mecca of Marfa. For the most part, you'll be traveling on I-10E for this journey.

The road from Joshua Tree to Phoenix is long, the desert expansive, the sight lines endless.

In L. A., set up camp at the Ace Hotel Downtown Los Angeles. Not only does the boutique hotel offer visual style by way of eclectic furnishings and Art Deco design, but the building is also the original home of the 1920s-era United Artists film studio.

A few blocks away at the contemporary art museum The Broad, you'll see a stellar lineup of rotating exhibits featuring works by Jean-Michel Basquiat and Roy Lichtenstein. Don't miss Yayoi Kusama's Infinity Mirror Rooms, a beguiling display of light and space. As you wander The Broad, take note of the building. Designed by Diller Scofidio + Renfro in collaboration with Gensler, it features a honeycomb-style structure that surrounds the "vault," an opaque mass hovering in the middle and serving as storage for the museum's collection.

To peruse literary works of art, visit The Last Bookstore. Notable as California's largest bookshop, the 22,000-square-foot (2,044-square-meter) reader's heaven takes a page from social media by designing visually appealing displays meant to attract Instagrammers.

Catch another showy display, this time by Mother Nature, with a sunset visit to Griffith Observatory. The panoramic views include L. A.,

Looking for a new handbag? You'll have to keep driving. While *Prada Marfa* near the tiny town of Valentine looks like a luxury fashion boutique, it's actually a permanent art installation. Swing by to see what's on display.

Hollywood, and the Pacific Ocean. It's from the Pacific that Sugarfish sources seafood for its traditional sushi—no California Rolls here. Another worthy dining option is Osteria Mozza, where James Beard Award-winning chef and La Brea Bakery founder Nancy Silverton perfects the art of (mozzarella) cheese.

Tear yourself away from the glamour of L.A. to cross the desert to Palm Springs. This sunny oasis boasts emerald golf courses and sapphire swimming pools, but more importantly, it's a suburban museum of some of the best mid-century architecture in the United States.

See for yourself on the Palm Springs Self-Guided Architecture Tour. Chart a course to architectural delights such as the Kaufmann Desert House by Richard Neutra; the Dinah Shore Residence and Royal Hawaiian Estates by Donald Wexler; and the Palm Springs Art Museum, Coachella Valley Savings and Loan (now Chase Bank), and Frank Sinatra Estate, all by E. Stewart Williams.

Retire for the evening at the Ace Hotel & Swim Club, but not before indulging in homemade pie and coffee in a leather booth at the hotel's retro diner, King's Highway.

Rested and refueled, it's time to hit the road to Joshua Tree. Here, two deserts merge into one glorious landscape where the Seussian Joshua tree (not a tree, in fact, but a yucca) reigns supreme. Have your camera handy to snap plenty of arty, sun-drenched pictures of its gnarled branches, then check out the Noah Purifoy Foundation.

The Alabama-born sculptor spent most of his life in the California desert. From 1989 to his death in 2004, Purifoy built the Outdoor Art Museum in Joshua Tree, an assemblage of more than 100 works of art on 10 acres (4 hectares) in the high desert. Take it all in, then get a bite to eat at chic La Copine and bed down at The Sea of Tranquility, a thoughtfully appointed lodging retreat owned by Italian filmmaker Tao Ruspoli.

The road from Joshua Tree to Phoenix is long, the desert expansive, the sight lines endless. As you near the fifth-largest city in the country, you'll spot that famous emblem of the West: the saguaro cactus. It grows only in the Sonoran Desert, a surprisingly lush ecosystem that thrives in Central and Southern Arizona, and Northern Mexico. Over the years, the saguaro →

New Mexico's 275 square miles (712 square kilometers) of pearly white pebbles, which compose the world's largest gypsum dune field, were designated as a national park in 2019. Hit the dunes for an otherworldly experience.

→ has made appearances in everything from Western films and Native American art to shirts and tea towels.

You might see the saguaro's depiction in the local art at Phoenix's Barrio Café. While you munch on chef Silvana Salcido Esparza's award-winning *cochinita pibil,* admire commissioned works by Lalo Cota, Lucinda Hinojos, Pablo Luna, and muralist Tato Caraveo.

Next, make the 30-minute drive from the heart of Phoenix to the hills of Scottsdale where legendary architect Frank Lloyd Wright once made his winter home at Taliesin West. Tour the grounds of this UNESCO World Heritage site to see Wright's innovative designs that blend the indoors and outdoors, mixing natural beauty with that made by man.

Another man-made wonder can be discovered just two hours south. Skirting the edges of Tucson sprawls Biosphere 2, dubbed the "world's largest science experiment." The open-to-the-public research facility is a glass-enclosed mini-Earth comprising natural environments like the ocean, rainforest, savanna, and more.

Check into Tucson's Hotel McCoy for the night. The restored motor lodge has been converted into an art hotel, where bold works adorn every surface: murals on the exterior walls, paintings for sale in the guest rooms, a lobby gallery.

As you make your way east to Marfa, you'll cross New Mexico. Stop at White Sands National Park in Alamogordo. It's one of the newest to join the national parks, and it shows off the world's

largest gypsum dune field—wave after undulating wave of bright, glittering sand.

The sun-cracked desert of West Texas shocks with its vastness. Unlike the Sonoran Desert, there's nary a plant to be found, save a dried tumbleweed or two. Which makes Prada Marfa all the more surprising. The art installation appears out of nowhere just before you reach the town of Valentine. It looks like a real Prada store, except it's never open and the shoes are all props. The artists Elmgreen and Dragset describe the installation as a "pop architectural land art project" meant to challenge society's relationship with consumerism.

As the road winds south, Marfa shimmers like a mirage in the distance. An arts hub, Marfa attracts big names in the film, music, →

It'll often happen that you take a look around and wonder if you've walked onto the set of a Western. Ghost towns, life-size sculptures, and regular tumbleweed crossings only reinforce the feeling. Saddle up, partner.

→ and visual arts world from London, New York, and Los Angeles.

It started when artist Donald Judd moved to Marfa in the 1970s, buying up abandoned buildings to house his works. Soon, other artists followed. Today, the Chinati Foundation and the Judd Foundation maintain Donald Judd's Marfa installations and archives. Sign up for a guided tour of his studios and large-scale architectural projects.

In downtown Marfa, stroll by art galleries featuring works that span a range of media: painting, photography, sculpture, textile, and performance art. Feel free to pop into any that are open, or call ahead for an appointment. If you're not sure where to start, the Marfa Gallery Guide available at the visitor center offers suggestions.

You have your pick of lodging at Marfa's El Cosmico, from bohemian yurts to glamping trailers. If you have your own tent stashed in the trunk, good news, El Cosmico has self-camping as well.

For sustenance, there's the rustic elegance and South American cuisine of Al Campo or the everything-handmade fare at Marfa Burrito. When night falls, grab a blanket and join the folks on the edge of town at the Marfa Lights Viewing Center. The dark skies of West Texas paint a deep indigo backdrop for the mysterious Marfa Lights—faint orbs that glow and bob on the dark horizon.

From Marfa, it's a desolate yet lovely drive to the ghost town of Terlingua. Like El Cosmico, Basecamp Terlingua lets you choose from myriad

sleeping options, though the "bubbles" are by far the best. These circular rooms sport see-through walls and ceilings to take advantage of the desert panorama, and some even include outdoor hot tubs and fire pits.

Enjoy dinner and a live Texas banjo at the Starlight Theatre Restaurant and Saloon before visiting nearby Big Bend National Park for stargazing. Big Bend is one of the largest national parks and it's known for its esteemed stargazing programs thanks to having the least light pollution of any national park in the Lower 48.

Joshua Tree artist Noah Purifoy once said: "I do not wish to be an artist, I only wish that art enables me to be." For this road trip, that sentiment rings true no matter if you're a talented maker or simply an art appreciator. ◆

Noah Purifoy once said:
"I do not wish to be
an artist, I only wish that
art enables me to be."
For this road trip, that
sentiment rings
true no matter if you're a
talented maker or simply
an art appreciator.

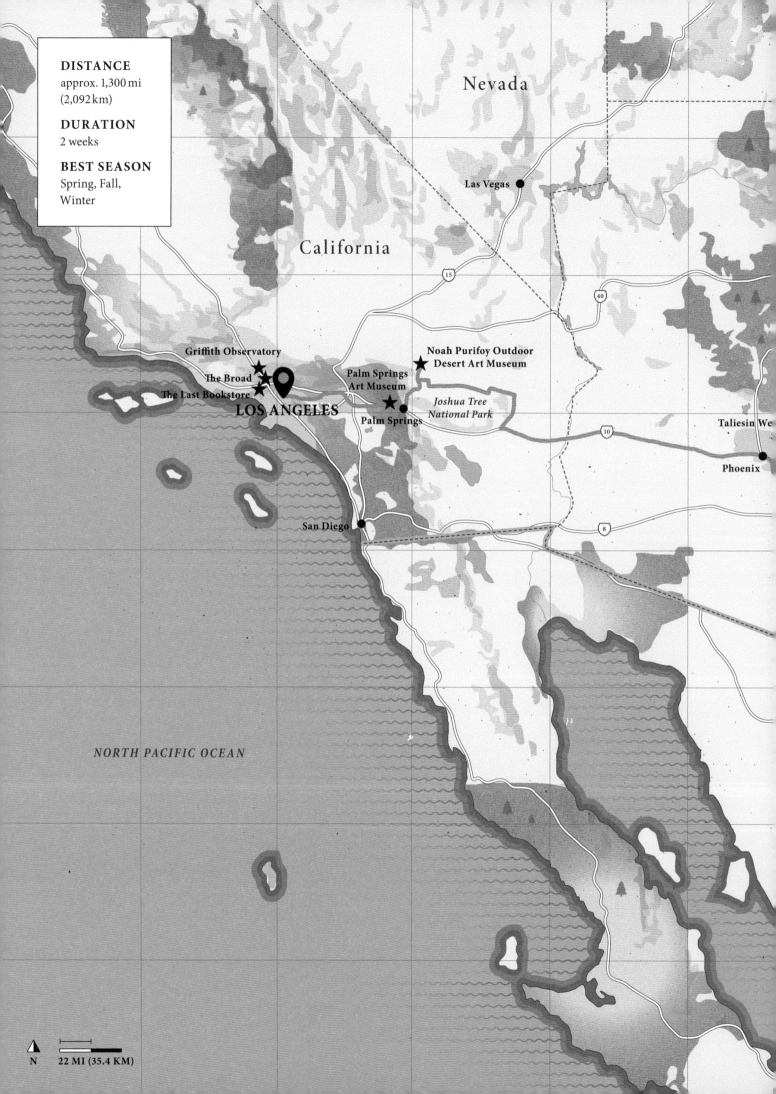

DISTANCE
approx. 1,300 mi
(2,092 km)

DURATION
2 weeks

BEST SEASON
Spring, Fall,
Winter

Nevada

Las Vegas

California

15

40

Griffith Observatory

The Broad

The Last Bookstore

LOS ANGELES

Palm Springs
Art Museum

Noah Purifoy Outdoor
Desert Art Museum

Joshua Tree
National Park

10

Taliesin We

Phoenix

Palm Springs

San Diego

8

NORTH PACIFIC OCEAN

N

22 MI (35.4 KM)

USA

Arizona

Biosphere 2

New Mexico

Texas

Albuquerque

White Sands
National Park

Alamogordo

ROUTE
ARCHITECTURE
AND ART

Prada Marfa

Judd Foundation

Chinati Foundation

Marfa Lights Viewing Center

MARFA

Terlingua

Big Bend
National Park

MEXICO

Indulge Your Whims in America's Fun-Filled, Party-Packed Vice Cities

MIAMI, FLORIDA → LAS VEGAS, NEVADA

Whether it's lazy days by the pool, eating decadent foods, or dancing until dawn, the goal of this trip: do exactly as you please.

Loosely defined as a bad habit, a vice can be anything from a penchant for sweets to the entire plot of *The Hangover* movie. And most people would agree that giving in to vices every now and then is fun. That's why there are destinations infamous for letting you revel in temptation. Las Vegas comes to mind, with its lineup of gambling, X-rated (and G-rated) shows, all-you-can-eat buffets, and 24-hour nightlife.

But hedonism can also skew mild, such as luxuriating at a spa or simply letting your freak flag fly. On this 2,700-mile (4,345-kilometer), three-week trip, try it all—at least once—from Miami to New Orleans, Austin, Scottsdale, and Las Vegas. In the mood to max out the vice life? Add a detour to hit up Atlanta.

But first, you start in vibrant Miami.

The number one rule of Miami: skip sleep. The party rages day and night.

Miami, Florida, is made for pleasure-seekers. Perhaps that's why it's called the Magic City. Year-round tropical weather. Candy-colored architecture. Latin music pulsing from clubs and the aroma of croquetas wafting from bakeries. The city buzzes—at DJ pool parties, in front of bold murals, in Cuban restaurants. No matter where you go, it's impossible not to soak up the live-wire energy.

The number one rule of Miami: skip sleep. The party rages day and night, moving from the beach to the club when the sun goes down. And at the popular nightspot Sweet Liberty, the fun doesn't end until the sun rises. Celebrity sightings are common at LIV and Bâoli, while ocean views and boozy cocktails are in style at rooftop bars like Astra, Sugar, and No. 3 Social.

Take a break from the dance floor to sample Miami's renowned Cuban cuisine in Little Havana. Your palate will love minty mojitos, guava pastries, and medianoche, a sandwich with ham, Swiss, and pickles. One of Miami's most famous residents, Gloria Estefan, owns Estefan Kitchen, which pairs the singer's childhood recipes with live entertainment. Before you leave, perfect your Miami tan with a little beach time.

A good reason to detour from the westerly trajectory of your trip: Atlanta, Georgia, if for nothing else than to stuff yourself with belly-warming Southern food.

Before hitting the Sin Cities, put in a few wholesome hours in Arizona's Painted Desert and among the giant saguaros. Then ask for an advance pardon at the San Xavier del Bac Mission just outside Tucson.

An interesting food fact about the ATL is that it's the birthplace of Coca-Cola. Atlanta celebrates its fizzy fame at the World of Coca-Cola Museum where, among other exhibits, you can see the vault where the soda's super-secret recipe is kept.

Then it's time to eat. And eat and eat. Virgil's cooks up excellent soul food like she-crab soup; fried lobster, shrimp, and fish; and red rice and collard greens. More soul food fills the menu (and hearty appetites) at K&K. Order biscuits and sausage or country-fried steak, or try something new with beef liver and chicken gizzards. When in Rome, right?

Though the ATL may be known for its cuisine, the city's music scene rivals that of L. A. and New York, and is notable for launching the careers of rap and hip-hop performers like Outkast, T. I., and Ludacris. Immerse yourself in the scene at the Midtown Music Fest, held every September. Then drive into the Deep South for your next destination.

New Orleans, Louisiana earned its nickname, the Big Easy, in the 1960s, a moniker distinguishing itself as the laid-back opposite to hustling, bustling New York, a k a the Big Apple. The easygoing vibe of New Orleans extends to every cobblestone corner of the city, from the lingering jazz notes on Frenchman Street to the locals' slow-rolling Creole accents—and to its anything-goes attitude. This is best experienced during Mardi Gras. At the March event's parades and parties, you'll see costumed performers waving from floats, beaded necklaces

flying through air, and drunk revelers swigging from takeaway cups in the streets. You'll hear marching bands and buskers. You'll smell warm beignets, and if you duck into the right restaurant (Frankie & Johnny's is a choice option), you'll savor the taste of boiled crawfish. French for "Fat Tuesday," Mardi Gras marks the last night before Lent and salutes the chance to eat, drink, and be merry before a season of fasting. If ever there was a time to give over to your impulses, it's on the eve of abstinence, no?

For a Mardi Gras-like atmosphere other times of the year, check out the French Quarter. It's the city's most historic neighborhood, one equally famous for its nightlife as for its wrought-iron balconies. Catch a show in the clubs on Bourbon Street or grab a bite to eat in a Cajun →

The "Overseas Highway" is a 113-mile (182-kilometer) joyride that connects Miami and Key West and brings you to one of the largest barrier reefs in the world. And where Scottsdale is decidedly Western, Austin is just plain weird.

→ restaurant. On your way out of town, take things down a notch with a stroll through the French Market.

Follow the Gulf Coast into Texas, traveling to the heart of the state. If you seek a safe haven to lean into your freaky side, you've found it in Austin. After all, the slogan is "Keep Austin Weird."

One of the city's many strange points of pride is also how Austin got the name Bat City. Every summer nearly 1.5 million Mexican free-tailed bats burst out from under Congress Bridge. It usually happens at sunset, and it's as beautiful and mesmerizing as it is spooky.

That blend of weird and wonderful shows up all over town. Join the festivity of oddities at places like Little Longhorn Saloon where a favorite pastime for bar patrons is to play a version of bingo that involves a chicken and its poop.

After all, the slogan is "Keep Austin Weird."

Then there's Banger's, a craft-beer garden that offers to tattoo their logo anywhere on your body—don't be shy, thousands of others have done it. Or how about the Cathedral of Junk, an art installation by local man Vince Hannemann comprising 60 tons of stuff: car bumpers, bottles, lawn mower parts, kitchen utensils, bicycle

wheels, and a whole lot more. Catch a live honky-tonk show and then go west across New Mexico and Arizona to Scottsdale.

While "Old Town" Scottsdale highlights its Western roots—country music at Rusty Spur Saloon, cowboy-art galleries—the rest of the city glimmers like Beverly Hills. Dozens of luxury resorts sprawl their manicured lawns and pamper guests with spa treatments, restaurants helmed by celebrity-chefs, and sparkling swimming pools where you can doze in between sips of bottomless mimosas.

Sanctuary Resort & Spa nestles against Camelback Mountain and rumored past guests include Beyoncé and Jay-Z. Take in the views from the floor-to-ceiling windows at Elements, the resort's pricey restaurant operated by Food →

While "Old Town" Scottsdale highlights its Western roots—country music at Rusty Spur Saloon, cowboy-art galleries—the rest of the city glimmers like Beverly Hills.

What's a trip to the desert without some craft brews and grape juice? And no, you haven't had a few too many—the Valley of Fire really does look like that. Don't be surprised if you come home with a Route 66 road sign to hang up in the garage.

→ Network chef Beau MacMillan. Nearby resorts include the Moroccan-themed oasis of Omni Montelucia, midcentury modern Mountain Shadows Resort, and elegant JW Marriott Camelback. In between massages and five-course brunches, make time to shop luxury brands like Gucci and Bulgari at Scottsdale Fashion Square.

Scottsdale is also home to the Phoenix Open, a celebrity-studded, fashion-forward, see-and-be-seen PGA golf tournament at the Fairmont Scottsdale Princess. Though officially a sporting event, the Phoenix Open is also a mini vice city all its own. Drinking starts before 8:00 a. m. and the white-tent parties—complete with DJs, dancing, and VIP lounges—go all night.

From Scottsdale, it's a five-hour drive to the ultimate destination for debauchery: Las Vegas. Otherwise known as Sin City, the City That Never Sleeps, the Gambling Capital of the World, the Entertainment Capital of the World…the list goes on.

Like the desert it calls home, Las Vegas is a city of extremes.

The city's past is riddled with stories of people who fell under the Vegas spell only to find themselves involved in quickie weddings, wild bachelor parties, epic gambling wins, and even more epic losses. Like the desert it calls home, Las Vegas is a city of extremes, one with no rules except to do whatever feels right in the moment.

As soon as you step onto the Strip, you're enveloped in the city's neon blanket. The Strip is where you'll find hotel casinos like Caesars Palace, The Bellagio, The Venetian, and MGM Grand, and it's a good starting point for a Vegas adventure. Each hotel offers numerous restaurants, shows, concerts, shopping, and of course, gambling. Since Las Vegas allows open containers, it's not frowned upon (then again, in Vegas, what is?) to grab a cocktail and walk from casino to casino, stopping to play a slot or a round of blackjack when it suits your fancy.

Las Vegas enjoyed its rise to popularity as a tourist destination under Mafia rule;

it was mobster Bugsy Siegel who opened the first resort-style hotel on the Strip before he was murdered in 1947. The Mob Museum offers a fascinating look at the link between Las Vegas and the mob and is a quiet spot to take a break from the never-ending party.

While you're here, whether you choose to unwind by the pool or close out your trip in true vice-city style with a two-day bender, consider this: in a world where we're constantly on the go, tethered to jobs, obligations, and routines, there's no harm in doing what makes you happy. Even if it's just for a short while. ◆

In a world where we're constantly on the go, tethered to jobs, obligations, and routines, there's no harm in doing what makes you happy.

DISTANCE
approx. 2,700 mi
(4,345 km)

DURATION
3 weeks

BEST SEASON
Spring, Fall,
Winter

Wyoming

Nebr

Salt Lake City

Denver

Utah

Colorado

Kansas

LAS VEGAS

Arizona

California

Los Angeles

Scottsdale

New Mexico

USA

Texas

ROUTE

VICE CITIES

MEXICO

N

47 MI (75.6 KM)

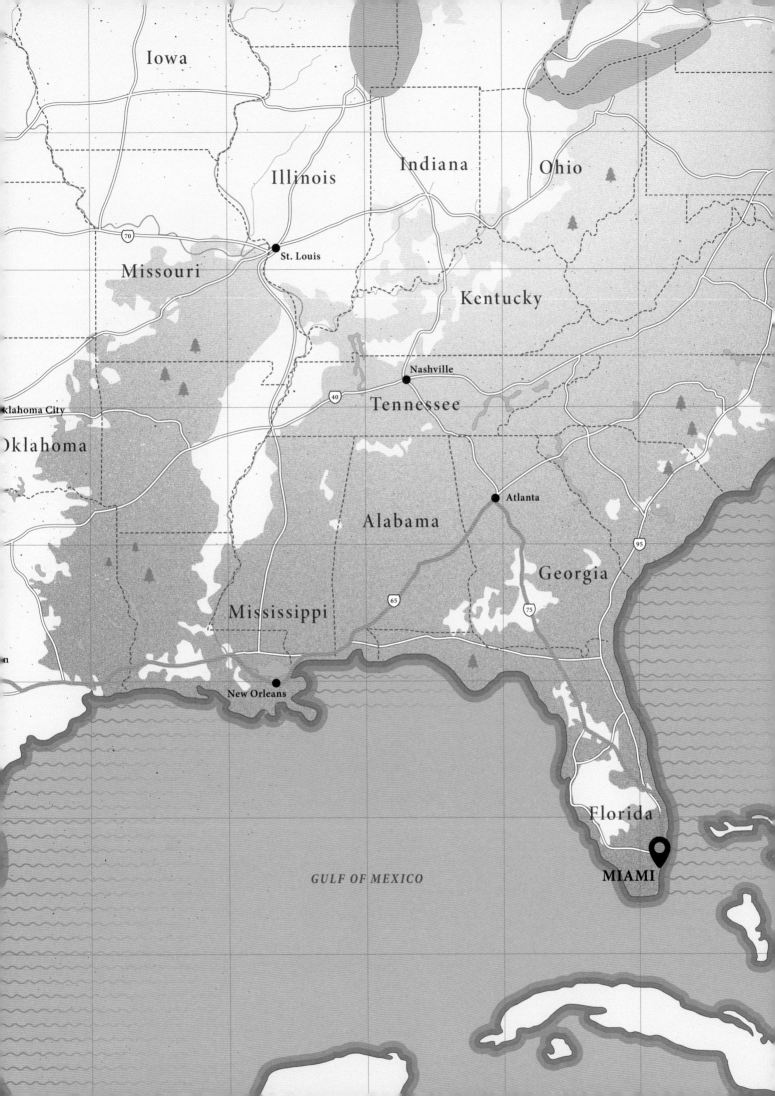

Ascend the Slopes: Enjoy the Powder and Peaks around Great Salt Lake

SALT LAKE CITY, UTAH

Salt Lake City's well-heeled downtown is a perfect base
for skiing and hiking in the surrounding mountains.

Thanks to its religious affiliations, Salt Lake City has had a reputation of being uptight and buttoned-down. However, the city's growing popularity as a base for fans of outdoor adventure means that "The Crossroads of the West" is quickly shedding its stodgy image. The range of recreational possibilities within an hour or so by car from downtown Salt Lake City is nothing short of exhilarating, with ski and snowboard resorts, and miles of scenic mountain trails for hiking, mountain biking, and horseback riding.

Whatever the pious undertones, you have to admit that Salt Lake City is pleasantly and conveniently organized as a destination. Downtown is clean, well-maintained, and family-friendly. The streets are a generous 132 feet (40 meters) wide; it is said that founder, town planner, and polygamist Brigham Young could walk down them comfortably arm in arm with all of his wives. You can warm up to more demanding physical exertions with a few laps around the beautiful Liberty Park, where children and dogs play on the lawns, and the songs of 400 species of bird can be caught on the breeze.

The range of activities around Salt Lake City is nothing short of exhilarating.

Liberty Park is also an unexpected place to find art, but find your way to the Chase Home Museum of Utah Folk Arts, where you can delight in exhibits of pioneer art, Native American art, and folk art. More famous names line up for appreciation within the walls of the Utah Museum of Fine Arts, where works by Brueghel, Van Dyck, and Rodin mix with masterpieces by Thomas Gainsborough and John Singer Sargent.

It would be a shame not to visit Great Salt Lake itself, a veritable ocean in the middle of the desert, itself a fraction of the huge Lake Bonneville that once covered huge swathes of western Utah as well as regions of Idaho and Nevada. With no outlets, the minerals that accumulate there stay there, and are frequently mined, but away from the industry, you can spot wildlife and migratory birds on the trails at Antelope Island State Park.

We're here to explore the great outdoors, though, with its promise of skiing and hiking. Take I-80 east as it snakes through the verdant

If the endless white starts to make you go snowblind, take a detour to eastern Utah where the town of Moab is your gateway to Arches National Park and its stunning red rock formations. Heading southwest, you'll enter the martian landscape of Canyonlands National Park with its iconic mesas and buttes carved by the Green and Colorado Rivers.

foothills of Mount Aire. The landscape out here is still relatively green and lush enough to sustain golf courses and country clubs. As the road steadily climbs, you'll find yourself at an elevation of 6,000 feet (1,829 meters) around Snyderville. From here it's a natural progression to head to any one of the region's ski resorts—Park City, Deer Valley, and Bald Eagle Mountain being the pick of the crop. Bask in the glorious personal space on the slopes at Deer Valley, where limited passes and high-speed lifts make for an unrushed, uncrushed experience.

Beyond the slopes, the vast expanse of Jordanelle State Park is ripe for exploration and is home to three major recreational areas, Hailstone, Rock Cliff, and Ross Creek. Hailstone

offers a return to nature, with campgrounds to return to after a day's fishing or canoeing, while Rock Cliff is a haven of tranquility, with nature trails for birders and photographers. Hikers, mountain bikers, and equestrians can adventure along the trails from Ross Creek, through the shady pathways in the beautiful aspen groves. In winter months, the park offers horse-drawn carriage rides through the snowy fields of dramatically illuminated trees.

UT-190 also leads eastwards out of the city, following the unpredictable twists of Big Cottonwood Creek as it negotiates the foothills of Mount Superior. Hiking trailheads pepper the route, leading to glassy lakes and scenic lookouts such as Twin Peaks Wilderness with its rugged terrain, narrow canyons, and the →

Not all that far from the desert, skyscraping peaks offer winter sports enthusiasts some of America's snowiest playgrounds. Take the Snowbird Aerial Tram to the top of Hidden Peak at 11,000 feet (3,353 meters), and marvel at the Salt Lake Valley below.

→ towering crests of O'Sullivan and Dromedary Peaks. The Lake Blanche Trail welcomes advanced hikers and rewards them with memorable views as they follow the pathways carved out by ancient glaciers over the millennia.

Waterfalls abound in this region, the most notable being Doughnut Falls, which is popular enough to merit its own hiking trailhead. It's a more casual walk, around 3.5 miles (5.6 kilometers) round trip, and features a unique rock formation that allows Big Cottonwood Creek to gush through a doughnut-shaped hole in the mountainside.

During ski season, your likely destination will be the resort of Solitude. Solitude averages 500 inches (12.7 meters) of snowfall per year and boasts over 1,200 acres (486 hectares) of skiable terrain. While this includes serious groomed runs, powder glades, and Nordic trails that will appeal to skilled skiers, there's a casual, family-friendly ambiance to Solitude.

There's nothing like taking in the slopes from above.

Beginners and less accomplished skiers can find their feet in the Moonbeam area. Meanwhile, adrenaline seekers can hop on the Summit Express lift to the glorious vistas of the Honeycomb Canyon with its rugged, challenging terrain.

Further south, UT-210 is a shorter road that also juts eastwards in the shadow of the south face of O'Sullivan Peak. The path here follows the smaller sibling, Little Cottonwood Creek, and gentle hiking trails along the way will lead you to the natural steps of Gloria Falls and the calm repose of Red Pine Lake and White Pine Lake.

Just beyond this bucolic countryside, Snowbird ski resort (in the equally well-named town of Alta) lives up to its name and enjoys the longest ski season in Utah—some reports even tell of skiing here on the 4th of July. A whopping 2,500 acres (1,012 hectares) of slopes and a 3,240-foot (988-meter) vertical drop keep the crowds coming, but for first-timers, there's nothing like taking in the slopes from above.

Snowbird's Aerial Tram whisks passengers along a 1.6-mile (2.6-kilometer) cable and up 2,900 vertical feet (884 vertical meters) in 10 minutes to the top of Hidden Peak. The views from the canyon will stay with you as you look out over Mount Superior, Peruvian Gulch, Gad Valley, and the Mineral Basin.

All of these regions are similarly spectacular during the spring and summer months, substituting skis for hiking boots or mountain bikes, and with trails for every skill level, everyone from young families to hard-nosed explorers can find their happy places. ◆

Antelope Island
State Park

GREAT SALT LAKE

Utah Muse
of Fine Ar

SALT LAKE CITY

Chase Home
Museum

Liberty Park

N

28 MI (45 KM)

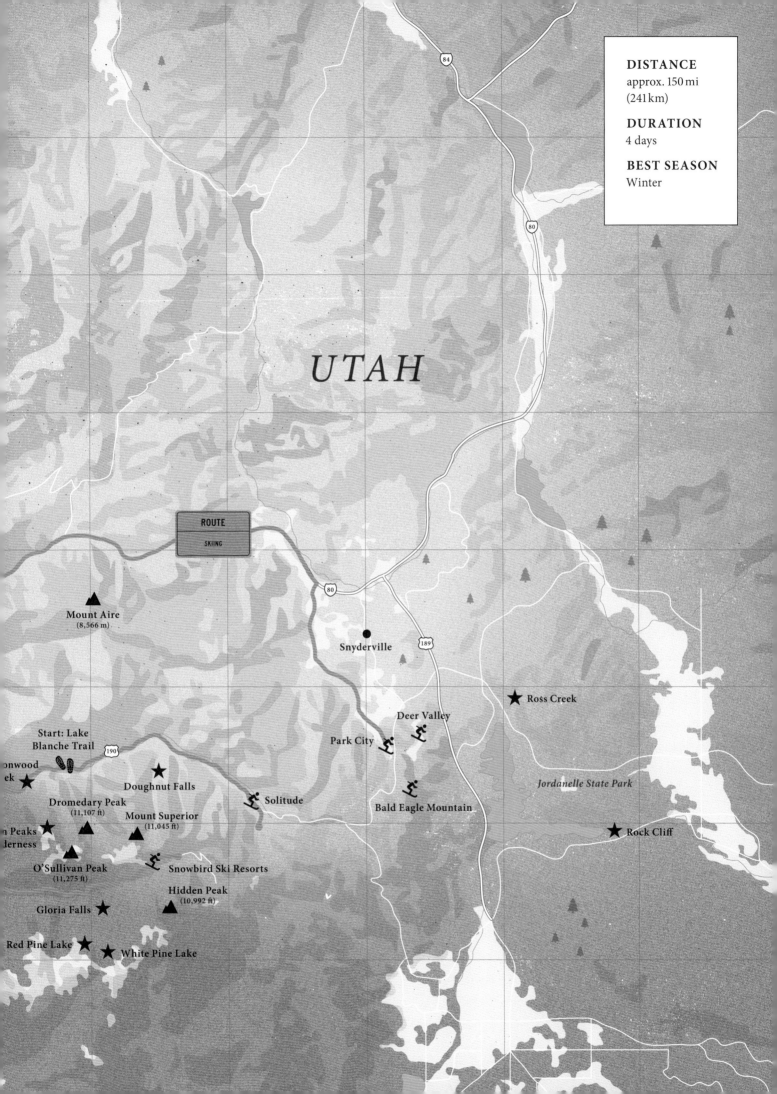

UTAH

84

80

80

189

Snyderville

★ Ross Creek

Mount Aire
(8,566 m)

Deer Valley

Park City

Start: Lake
Blanche Trail

190

Doughnut Falls

Jordanelle State Park

onwood
k ★

★

Solitude

Bald Eagle Mountain

Dromedary Peak
(11,107 ft)

Mount Superior
(11,045 ft)

Peaks
lerness ★

★ Rock Cliff

O'Sullivan Peak
(11,275 ft)

Snowbird Ski Resorts

Hidden Peak
(10,992 ft)

Gloria Falls ★

Red Pine Lake ★

★ White Pine Lake

ROUTE

SKIING

DISTANCE
approx. 150 mi
(241 km)

DURATION
4 days

BEST SEASON
Winter

Witness the Winding Mountain Roads of Colorado's Mile-High Splendor

DENVER, COLORADO → WOLF CREEK, COLORADO

Ski resorts, historic mining towns, and a series of spectacular drives await on this elevated road trip.

The Top of the Rockies Byway, one of the highest in the United States, spans 82 miles (132 kilometers) between Copper Mountain and Leadville and almost never drops below the 9,000-foot (2,743-meter) mark. Just a little warning for those prone to altitude sickness.

Finding a sturdy set of wheels for the spectacular 600 miles (966 kilometers) of mountain roads ahead should be your first priority as you arrive in Denver, Colorado. The Mile High City doesn't have its origins in the convenience of a riverside or coastal location; it was born from the hard slog of mining gold and minerals. It's an easy-going destination these days, though, and you can enjoy the backdrop of the Rocky Mountains while wandering among the historic redbrick buildings of Lower Downtown and Larimer Square.

Once you've acclimated to the elevation and have outfitted yourself with some warm clothes, join I-70, which snakes westward into the foothills. An hour from the city, the vertiginous splendor of the Mount Evans Scenic Byway beckons. This is the highest paved road in North America, open to vehicles from Memorial Day to Labor Day.

Get ready for the highest paved road in North America.

The entire road climbs 9,000 feet (2,743 meters) through five climate zones in one hour of driving, curling through the high plains and rewarding determined motorists with summit views from Mount Evans at just over 14,000 feet (4,267 meters). Breathe in air that's likely as clean as you've ever known, and survey the vista before

you, from Never Summer Range in the north to the Sangre de Cristo Mountains in the south.

Parts of Breckenridge form a modern ski resort, but its historic district boasts structures that have somehow survived the 160 years or so since it was a rough-hewn, log cabin town along the Blue River. Colorfully evocative Victorian buildings stand out against the gray and white of the Rocky Mountains' Tenmile Range. Both the Pollock House and Chinese Laundry House stand almost exactly as they were in 1862, when the first roads and shacks made up a burgeoning but lawless mining town. There's even a strange, small museum here, the Edwin Carter Museum, filled with wildlife from the Central Rockies, caught and preserved via taxidermy in the mid-19th century.

Spring, summer, and fall are by far the best times to explore the Top of the Rockies Scenic Byway and Independence Pass, severe winter weather often shutting down sections of this spectacular drive. The roads twist through the hills surrounding Colorado's two loftiest mountains, Elbert and Massive. Fortunes were made here in the 19th century, and small communities survive to this day. Independence Pass is open from May through early November each year, and driving 12,000 feet (3,658 meters) above sea level with the panoramic alpine tundra on both sides is one of the country's truly breathtaking drives.

Powderheads will feel their senses awakening as the region's best-known ski resorts start to come into view. The historic homes and →

→ rickety shacks of yesteryear give way to the posh chalets and high-end ski culture of Aspen, its four resorts attracting 1.5 million visitors every year. You can avoid the crowds by seeing some of the lesser-known attractions, though. Learn about the city's origins in tin mining at the Smuggler Mine, with a tour that delves some 1,200 feet (366 meters) underground. You can also wander around neighboring Ashcroft Ghost Town, where an abandoned saloon, post office, and hotel are the last remnants of a 19th-century outpost.

Leaving Aspen, you'll be following the route of early Colorado Midland Railroad routes from the city to Glenwood Springs. Basalt Mountain looms to the northeast, the steep valley floor eventually widening and opening up to increasingly lush fields and farming communities, ranches zipping by as Carbondale's suburbs arrive.

In Aspen, shacks of yesteryear give way to posh chalets and high-end ski culture.

The seasonal Kebler Pass awaits, though, connecting Crested Butte with Paonia. The drive takes nearly two hours at an average elevation of 10,000 feet (3,048 meters) through awe-inspiring alpine terrain. The peaks of Gunnison National Park and beyond tower in the distance as you pass through the region's largest aspen groves and the evergreen forests of the West Elk Mountains (though avoid the severe winter months for full access).

From the town of Gunnison, follow its namesake river west once more, where a series of huge reservoirs define the landscape. The still waters of the Curecanti National Recreation Area attract anglers from around the country looking to catch salmon or trout, and you can find some welcome tranquility in the off-grid network of campsites.

An hour or so further on US-50 and your Wild West, pioneering fantasies can play out. In Montrose, Colorado, the Old West comes to life at the Museum of the Mountain West. Twenty-five authentic historic buildings create a cinematic experience, evoking the border towns of the Gold Rush era. A saloon and dry goods store stand with the 1913 German Lutheran Church and the 1882 Denver & Rio Grande Railroad

The mighty Rocky Mountains serve as the backdrop for almost every mile of this long and winding route. It's a biker's dream and equally awesome for #vanlife. Pack your cowboy hat and discover why they still call it the Wild West.

section house, and some 500,000 genuine artifacts complete the century-old ambiance.

Connecting Ouray and Silverton, the so-called Million Dollar Highway awaits, though there's some dispute about how it got its name. Some say it was originally such a risky route that drivers said they wouldn't use it for a million dollars; other stories claim that it reputedly cost a million dollars per mile to build. In any case, the views of the valleys, peaks, and gorges of the San Juan Mountains verge on priceless. The road is open year-round, but you'll need chains in the harsher winter months.

In the late 1800s, Telluride had more per capita wealth than Manhattan, and it was the first city in the world to have alternating current (AC) power. There are legacies of its well-to-do past, such as the Sheridan Opera House, a performing-arts venue dating back to 1913. The elevation levels here hold a number of notable records—Telluride Regional Airport is the highest commercial airport in North America (9,078 feet/2,767 meters) and Alpino Vino is the highest restaurant in North America (11,996 feet/3,656 meters).

You'll step even further back into history an hour's drive southwest. Cortez is one of America's richest archaeological centers and neighbors the world-famous Mesa Verde National Park and the Ute Mountain Tribal Park. The Ancestral Pueblo people built thriving communities on the mesas here for over seven centuries, and it's humbling to see the ancient cliff dwellings that have been preserved here, as well as the many Native American artifacts at the Chapin Mesa Archeological Museum.

A straight shot west for a couple of hours along US-160 and the fringes of the San Juan National Forest delivers one last view of high-desert mesas and alpine peaks. The end of the trail is Wolf Creek, which boasts "the most snow in Colorado" with some 430 inches (1,092 centimeters) per year. The nearby hot springs of Pagosa offer a final, soothing respite from the demands of hiking or snowboarding, and you can savor the memories of this high-wire road trip as you soak. ◆

The still waters of the Curecanti National Recreation Area attract anglers from around the country looking to catch salmon or trout, and you can find some welcome tranquility in the off-grid network of campsites.

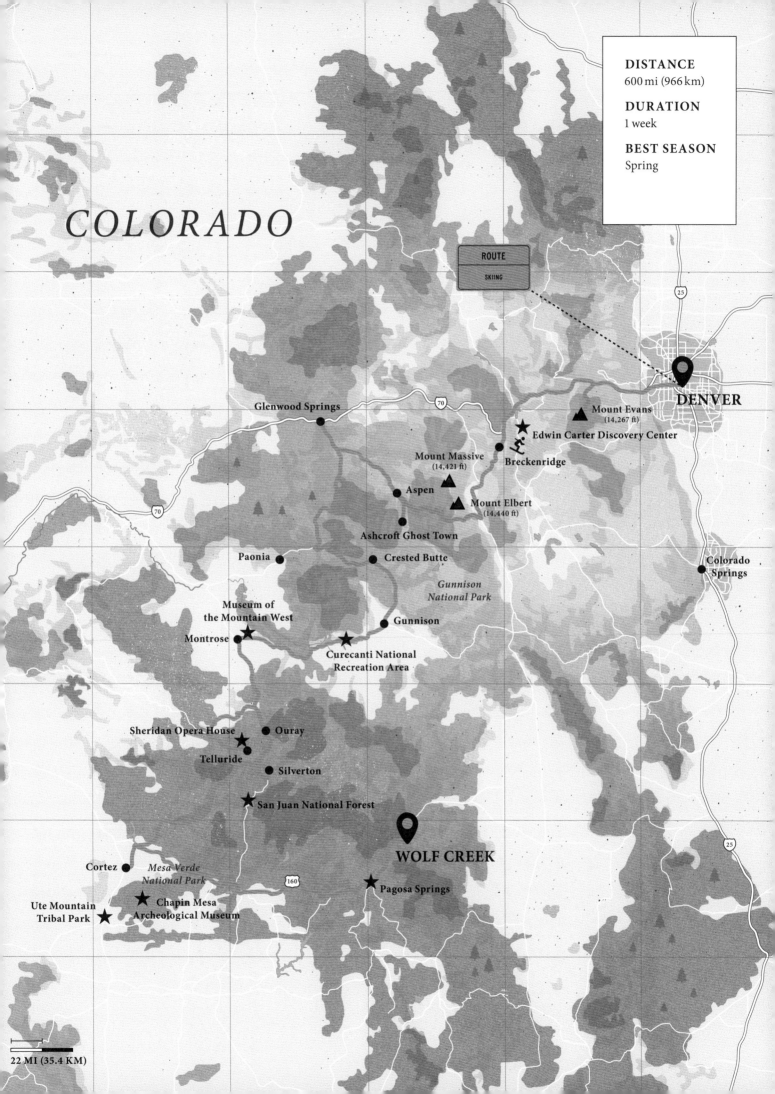

COLORADO

DISTANCE
600 mi (966 km)

DURATION
1 week

BEST SEASON
Spring

ROUTE

SKIING

DENVER

Mount Evans
(14,267 ft)

Glenwood Springs

Edwin Carter Discovery Center

Mount Massive
(14,421 ft)

Breckenridge

Aspen

Mount Elbert
(14,440 ft)

Ashcroft Ghost Town

Paonia

Crested Butte

Colorado
Springs

Gunnison
National Park

Museum of
the Mountain West

Gunnison

Montrose

Curecanti National
Recreation Area

Sheridan Opera House

Ouray

Telluride

Silverton

San Juan National Forest

WOLF CREEK

Cortez

Mesa Verde
National Park

Pagosa Springs

Ute Mountain
Tribal Park

Chapin Mesa
Archeological Museum

22 MI (35.4 KM)

Embark On an Adventure in Yellowstone and the Grand Tetons

JACKSON HOLE, WYOMING →
MAMMOTH, WYOMING

So much for the burden of choice. Discover two of America's most treasured national parks in a single trip.

Who hasn't dreamed of visiting Yellowstone? The park's 3,500 square miles (9,065 square kilometers) of raw wilderness spill into three states—Wyoming, Montana, and Idaho—and have enchanted natives, explorers, and visitors for more than 11,000 years. And with Grand Teton just a couple hours away, there's no excuse for not going back-to-back on this national park road tour. It's best to go in April or May and ideally with an SUV, though you won't have any trouble in smaller vehicles. However, with so many amazing hiking trails and camping spots to choose from, you'll be sorry if you don't load up and stay awhile.

Artist Point offers park visitors a breathtaking view of the Grand Canyon of the Yellowstone and Upper Falls. Bison herds frequently roam on, along, or across even busy roads, as they do here near Norris Geyser Basin.

The backbone of this route is U.S. Highway 191, which is Americana to the bone.

You can weave and wind your way through the region however you feel, taking anywhere from a few days to a few weeks. For the sake of brevity, we've mapped roughly 190 miles (306 kilometers). The backbone of this route is U.S. Highway 191, which is Americana to the bone: open skies, rolling fields, mountain backdrops, and the unparalleled freedom of being on the road.

Jackson Hole is as good a place to start as any, and no visit here would be complete without perusing the collection at The National Museum of Wildlife Art. Have a low-fuss lunch at the family-owned Virginian or take things up a notch by booking a table at Snake River Grill's upscale log cabin restaurant for dinner. Sleeping arrangements can be made at the true-to-surroundings Wyoming Inn. For breakfast, fuel up at Cafe Genevieve before hitting the road en route to Taggart Lake. But first, make a slight detour for the T. A. Moulton Barn, an early 20th-century Mormon homestead that seems staged for postcards.

The first stretch of the road trip is most beautiful along Teton Park Road, which runs parallel to US-191, though much closer to the mountains and lakes. Take that until you reach Taggart Lake and its eponymous trail loop, a 3.8-mile (6.1-kilometer) hike suitable for all skill levels. It'll bring you to the shores of two pristine alpine lakes with exceptional views of the mighty Grand Teton. Your next point of interest is just a short drive from here, at Jenny Lake, where the Cascade Canyon Trail takes you into moose territory and toward the peaks of Table Mountain. Back closer to sea level, have a bite at the Jenny Lake Lodge and consider spending the night before getting back on the road for day two.

The rest of Teton Park road takes you through sprawling flatlands and around the southern third of Jackson Lake before meeting up again with US-191. Shortly before the intersection, you'll see a right turn onto Signal →

Famed for its geysers,
mammal diversity,
and bison traffic jams,
Yellowstone really needs
no introduction.

The late CBS correspondent Charles Kuralt once called the Beartooth Highway "the most beautiful drive in America." Covering 70 miles (113 kilometers) and peaking at 10,947 feet (3,337 meters), it serves as the perfect gateway to Yellowstone from the northeast.

→ Mountain Road, which leads to an awesome panoramic summit at 7,720 feet (2,353 meters). Definitely worth a stop at the top. The next noteworthy vista awaits at the Oxbow Bend, which is peak Grand Teton as far as views go. Further up Jackson Lake, you'll find two splendid campsites, one at Colter Bay and the other at Lizard Creek. Is there anything better than falling asleep under the stars on the shores of a lake across from the mountains?

After Jackson Lake, you'll exit Grand Teton and enter a short no-man's-land before passing into Yellowstone, the world's oldest national park. Famed for its geysers, mammal diversity, and bison traffic jams, Yellowstone really needs no introduction. US-191 takes you to pretty much all the hot spots—literally—so

there's no need to worry about missing a turn. Check out the hydrothermal activity around the Norris Porcelain Basin if you don't want to deal with the crowds at the iconic Old Faithful.

US-191 (literally) takes you to all the hot spots.

Other standout hot springs include the vibrant Morning Glory Pool and the Grand Prismatic Spring. You'll also be happy to know that Yellowstone has its very own Grand Canyon, so you can respectfully move Arizona down your bucket list. Walk Uncle Tom's Trail for

the best views of the dramatic gorge and rapids and then head to the Brink of the Upper Falls for good measure.

Take US-191 long enough and you'll reach a point where it forks into US-89. Continue on US-89 and wind through some barren stretches until you reach a resting point at Gibbon Falls. The next batch of hot springs awaits at the appropriately named Geyser Creek, from which you can walk to the Artists Paintpots. After that, you can look forward to an absolute dream of a drive to the terminus of our itinerary, Mammoth, which is known for its terrace-like cascade of steaming travertine pools. And while we're getting out here, keep in mind Mammoth's still ages away from civilization. The journey continues… ◆

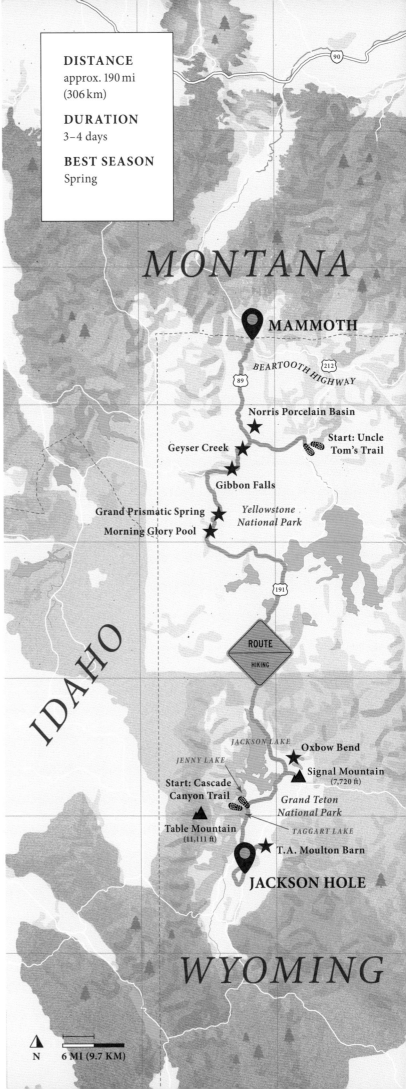

DISTANCE
approx. 190 mi
(306 km)

DURATION
3–4 days

BEST SEASON
Spring

MONTANA

MAMMOTH

BEARTOOTH HIGHWAY 212

89

Norris Porcelain Basin ★

Geyser Creek ★ ★ Start: Uncle
Tom's Trail

★ Gibbon Falls

Grand Prismatic Spring ★ *Yellowstone
National Park*

Morning Glory Pool ★

191

ROUTE

HIKING

IDAHO

JACKSON LAKE Oxbow Bend ★

JENNY LAKE ▲ Signal Mountain
(7,720 ft)

Start: Cascade
Canyon Trail *Grand Teton
National Park*

▲
Table Mountain *TAGGART LAKE*
(11,111 ft)

★ T.A. Moulton Barn

JACKSON HOLE

WYOMING

N
6 MI (9.7 KM)

Hug the Rockies in Glacier National Park

WEST GLACIER, MONTANA →
SAINT MARY, MONTANA

From icy peaks to pristine lakes, this 50-mile stretch is blessed with more photo ops than you can shake a camera at.

Going to the Sun Road may be the most aptly named route in America. It rises, and rises, and rises...all the way to 6,646 feet (2,026 meters). Along the way, you'll traverse the famed Logan Pass, from where you have a stunning view of more than a dozen snowcapped peaks.

One of the most memorable scenes in the 1994 road trip comedy *Dumb & Dumber* unfolds when the two protagonists, Harry and Lloyd, take a wrong turn on the way to the Rocky Mountains and land in the wheatfields of Nebraska. Their dismay leads Lloyd to declare, "That John Denver is full of shit, man," a reference to the song "Rocky Mountain High," in which the singer croons about "cathedral mountains," "silver clouds below," and a "fire in the sky." For your own Rocky adventure, you'll find no wrong turns on the Going-to-the-Sun Road.

Most travelers say there's something special about going west to east, from West Glacier to Saint Mary.

This stretch of humbling alpinescapes covers just a small fraction of Montana's Glacier National Park and is only open for several months a year owing to legendary snowdrifts that occur pretty much every season except summer. Best to plan a trip between July and September or, if you're aiming for the shoulder period on either side of that window, to check the forecast ahead of time. As the National Park Service notes, "predicting the precise opening date of Going-to-the-Sun Road is impossible." Last bit of business before moving on to the fun stuff: admission to the road is restricted to vehicles under 21 feet (6.4 meters) long, under 8 feet (2.4 meters) wide, and less than 10 feet (3 meters) tall. Not in the mood to measure? Take a motorcycle and you won't have to worry about any of that.

While you'll enjoy the journey going in either direction, most travelers say there's something special about going west to east, from West Glacier to Saint Mary. Doing it that way also sets you up with more food and drink options at the finish line. The road's many twists make for slow driving, which is all the better, considering the perpetuity of breathtaking sights. This being Glacier National Park, the main draw is, of course, the snowcapped peaks. Mount Siyeh is the tallest, at just over 10,000 feet (3,048 meters), while Going-to-the-Sun Mountain is the most imposing. The highest you'll get is the Logan Pass (6,646 feet/2,026 meters), which straddles the Continental Divide and snakes through the aforementioned peaks, plus about a dozen others that are no less worthy of mention. Eventually, you'll arrive at Saint Mary Lake, which has a cameo in *Forrest Gump*—another iconic comedy from 1994—and is also featured in the opening scene of Stanley Kubrick's *The Shining.* If you have the fortune of arriving on a clear day, expect to see, in Forrest's words, "two skies, one on top of the other."

If you're just passing through, the Going-to-the-Sun Road can be conquered in a couple of hours. Totally cool to do it that way, considering how much more park there is to explore. That said, there's enough to do over the 50-mile (80-kilometer) route to make a day of it. →

Plan a trip between July and September or, if you're aiming for the shoulder period on either side of that window, check the forecast ahead of time.

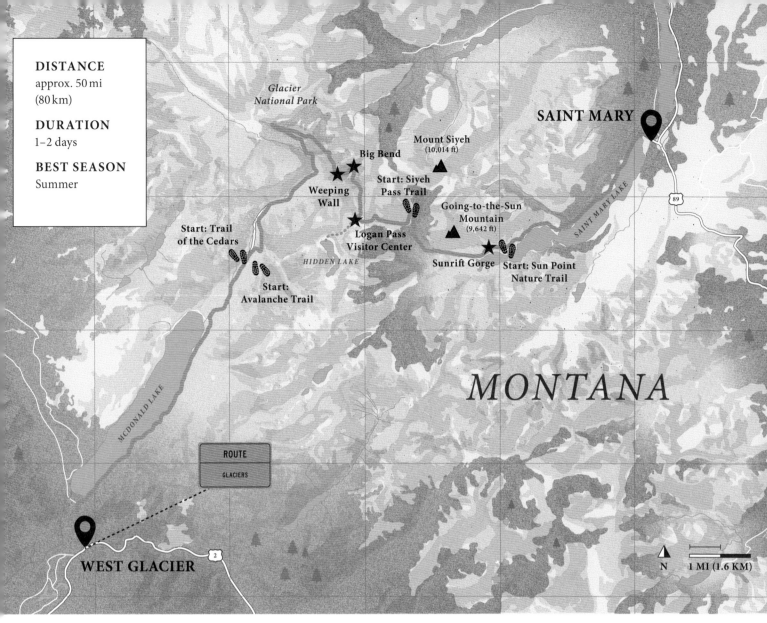

DISTANCE
approx. 50 mi
(80 km)

DURATION
1–2 days

BEST SEASON
Summer

Glacier National Park

SAINT MARY

Big Bend

Mount Siyeh
(10,014 ft)

Weeping Wall

Start: Siyeh Pass Trail

Going-to-the-Sun Mountain
(9,642 ft)

Start: Trail of the Cedars

Logan Pass Visitor Center

HIDDEN LAKE

Sunrift Gorge

Start: Sun Point Nature Trail

Start: Avalanche Trail

MCDONALD LAKE

MONTANA

SAINT MARY LAKE

89

ROUTE

GLACIERS

WEST GLACIER

2

N   1 MI (1.6 KM)

Covering more than a million acres, Glacier National Park is home to more than 130 named lakes, more than 1,000 different species of plants, hundreds of species of animals, and two different mountain ranges belonging to the Rockies.

→ Hidden Lake is probably about as wonderous a vista as you'll find anywhere in America. Evidently, many mountain goats agree. You can hike there from Logan Pass Visitor Center should you be among the lucky to land a parking spot.

Alternatively—well, there aren't many alternatives. The road's fame and short season mean you may have to forgo the hot spots and take a hike, literally. A walk around Lake McDonald with its rainbow pebbles is nothing short of fantastic, and you could even post up at one of several campgrounds—Sprague Creek or Fish Creek or even Backcountry—for a multiday adventure. Other notable hikes include the Siyeh Pass Trail, the Sun Point Nature Trail, the Trail of the Cedars, and the Avalanche Trail, the

latter of which leads to the piercing Avalanche Lake and, crucially, not to actual avalanches.

There's so much to see on this short road trip that you might run out of patience with your fellow passengers imploring you to keep your eyes on the road.

Check out Big Bend for the best sunset.

One thing you won't run out of is superlatives—greatest, prettiest, most astonishing. In that vein, check out Big Bend for the best sunset, traverse the Sunrift Gorge for the best waterfalls, and pass

through the Weeping Wall for the best (natural) car wash. Of course, it would be a disservice to put any of the wonders you'll encounter along the Going-to-the-Sun Road into superlative terms as they are, simply put, incomparable. ◆

Swap Sled Dogs for Horsepower on This Alaskan Adventure

ANCHORAGE, ALASKA

The national parks and glaciers that surround Anchorage
make for an exciting road trip into the wilderness.

G laciers and gold rushes have both shaped the landscape and infrastructure of this beautiful region, and seeing remote towns and national parks is easier than ever. You don't even need a pack of dogs and a sled these days, just a full tank of gas and some of that pioneering spirit. The climate here means that the warmer weeks from June through August are by far the best time to explore.

Modern-day Anchorage—the Alaskan capital—lies in a location with a long history of human habitation. In fact, there have been people here for around 10,000 years, with various Indigenous peoples coexisting until the arrival of James Cook in 1778. Formerly a part of Russia (the United States purchased Alaska in 1867), the town has been a trading post, gold rush center, and now has a diverse population of around 300,000 people.

The landscape here is virtually unchanged and, with the exception of the highway, has looked this way for thousands of years.

It's also a perfect base from which to explore the vast stretches of natural beauty that form the explorable parts of the surrounding countryside. Rent a 4WD or similarly sturdy vehicle, pack plenty of layers and warm clothes, and you'll be rewarded with spectacular views of glaciers, waterfalls, rock formations, and national parks.

Just north of the city is Eklutna Historical Park. Eklutna itself is a village which was founded in 1650 and remains the oldest continually inhabited village in the region. Its history means that both Indigenous peoples and Russian settlers have had a huge influence on the local culture, illustrated by the domed Russian Orthodox Church and the colorful "spirit houses" in the neighboring cemetery. From here, you can take a 3-mile (5-kilometer) round-trip hike to the scenic, 200-foot (61-meter) Thunderbird Falls, which freeze in the winter months to dramatic effect.

Travel 90 minutes northeast on AK-1 and traces of human habitation become less apparent by the mile. The landscape here is virtually →

Completed in 1942, the 1,700-mile (2,736-kilometer) Alaska Highway provided many Americans with their first real chance to explore the country's largest state. Just make sure to pack your passport if you plan on driving the whole route, as a large section of it cuts through Canada.

→ unchanged and, with the exception of the highway, has looked this way for thousands of years. Keep an eye out for moose who come to drink from the banks of the Matanuska River.

The valleys and hills in this area have been shaped over millennia by the Matanuska Glacier, which you can still see to this day. Head to the Matanuska Glacier State Recreation Site and take the gentle, 20-minute walk along the Edge Nature Trail, which leads through a shady forest to glacier viewing platforms.

The Matanuska Glacier is part of a huge ice field that's almost 100 miles (161 kilometers) across. You can drive around it in three hours or so and find yourself at an equally breath-taking spot, the Worthington Glacier. The Worthington Glacier State Recreation Site also

has easily accessible viewing spots, and this 4-mile- (6.4-kilometer-) long glacier stretches its fingers almost down to the roadway. Snowfall in this area is extremely high, accumulating up to 80 feet (24 meters) annually.

Doubling back, you can divert from the loop for an overnight adventure. You'll have to leave your vehicle in Chitina—driving onwards is possible in the warmer months, but even then the road is riddled with potholes, and it's nine hours of bumpy torture. Instead, catch a "bush flight" to McCarthy-Kennicott.

These former twin mining towns are located deep inside the country's largest national park, Wrangell–St. Elias. A former bordello turned modern-day inn called Ma Johnson's House provides the lodging, and the surrounding

nature provides the menu. McCarthy-Kennicott has a surprisingly dynamic culinary scene, with fresh-caught Copper River red salmon at the top of most people's wish list. Half-day glacier treks and copper mine tours can both help you build up an appetite.

Back on the original trail and back in your vehicle, you'll join the Richardson Highway—Alaska's oldest, which had its origins as a gold rush trail in the late 19th century. If you had driven this road a hundred years ago, you would have had the choice of dozens of road-houses, but these days there are just four, the pick of which might be Meier's Lake Roadhouse in Gakona, with its homemade comfort food and small museum of Athabascan Native American artifacts. →

Dozens of roadhouses sprung up during the Gold Rush of the early 1900s. And while many have since been boarded up or face a fragile future, there are still a few kicking around, serving a taste of Old Alaska. Definitely stop into The Sluice Box Bar at Mile 82 of the Denali Highway if you're in the area.

→ The road back to Anchorage has increasing amenities for travelers, most of them geared toward the appreciation of the outstanding Denali National Park, Alaska's most-visited national park. The views across the Nenana River Canyon with the Alaska Range mountains as a backdrop are truly memorable, especially if you're lucky enough to see the majestic caribou or moose on the slopes.

You might spot marmots, foxes, or dam-building beavers on the relatively easy Horseshoe Lake Trail, which meanders through the park for 3 miles (4.8 kilometers) or so. The Savage River Loop is just 1 mile (1.6 kilometers) long, but delivers stunning vistas of the canyon between Mount Margaret to the west and Healy Ridge to the east.

Pioneers and prospectors in the days before motor vehicles would, of course, rely on packs of sled dogs to transport them and their equipment through the snowy terrain. Denali is the only national park with its own kennel of sled dogs, and each year the park aims to breed or adopt one litter. You can see these hard-working dogs show off their skills during the summer months when rangers give daily demonstrations.

The most famous association with these special animals is the Iditarod Trail Sled Dog Race, a long-distance sled dog race run annually every March since 1973. You can experience a slice of this fascinating part of Alaskan culture at the Iditarod Museum, housed in the Sled Dog Race Headquarters in Wasilla, less than an hour outside of Anchorage. Video exhibits show the

challenges that the "mushers" (sled drivers) face in the grueling 1,049-mile (1,688-kilometer) race.

Back in Anchorage, the comforts of city life await, including a diversity of food choices that you likely haven't seen in a good few days. One of the most unexpected options is probably Hula Hands, a micro chain (there are two branches currently) that serves Hawaiian, Samoan, and Tongan dishes. Order some lomi salmon, or kalua pig, and feel transported to an island paradise, even if it's snowing outside. For unbeatable refreshment, though, Beluga Point Freshwater Spring just south of the capital has pure, Alaskan water straight from the source. ◆

ALASKA

DISTANCE
approx. 1,050 mi
(1,690 km)

DURATION
10 days

BEST SEASON
Summer

Nenana
River Canyon

③

②

Mount Margaret
(5,069 ft)

Start: Horseshoe
Lake Trail

Denali National Park

①

Gakona

Wrangell-St. Elias
National Park

Matanuska Glacier
State Recreation Site

MATANUSKA RIVER

Matanuska
Glacier

Chitina

McCarthy-Kennicott

Iditarod
Museum

Eklutna Historical Park

ROUTE

NATURE

Thunderbird Falls

Worthington
Glacier

ANCHORAGE

Worthington Glacier
State Recreational Site

12 MI (19.3 KM)

Slip Into a Sanctuary of Solitude: Behold the Wilderness around Seattle and Portland

PORTLAND, OREGON →
SEATTLE, WASHINGTON

Discover some of America's most breathtaking nature sandwiched between the Pacific Northwest's two largest cities.

No book on road trips would be complete without touching on the Pacific Northwest (PNW). And that's all this is, really: a touch. So expansive is the wondrous nature in, around, and between Portland and Seattle that everything from here on out should be considered written in sand not stone. Plan to cover around 700 miles (1,127 kilometers) over the course of 10 days in late summer/early fall, starting in Portland.

You don't even need to set foot in Seattle or Portland to understand the appeal of the Pacific Northwest's two largest cities. Namely, their proximity to the great outdoors. Just a few miles outside city limits and you're already deep in the greenery.

Stretch your legs with a stroll around Mirror Lake and listen to the rushing water of Little Zigzag Falls.

Now, there's a lot to say about Portland, so we'll keep it brief. The Japanese Garden is worth a stroll, the tacos from ¿Por Qué No? are a must, and a sugar rush from Voodoo Doughnut should probably be in the cards as well. Book a bed at the downtown Jupiter Hotel and you'll be within walking distance of all the other essentials. The next morning, see what's oven-fresh at St. Honoré Bakery before hitting the road and leaving the city behind.

The first stop is Mount Hood National Forest, named after a potentially active volcano

that you'll just have to trust will stay calm during your visit. Stretch your legs with a stroll around Mirror Lake and listen to the rushing water of Little Zigzag Falls. Then cap off your effort with a small-batch ale or two at the nearby Mt. Hood Brewing Co. Post-brew, consider hitting some trails—there are around 150 to choose from. Equally abundant are lodging options, from swanky cabins to bare-bones campgrounds. Look no further than the Huckleberry Inn for authentic mountain digs and dining.

The next stop is Bridal Veil, a ghost town on the Columbia River known for the falling cloak of water after which it is named. I-84 will get you there fastest, but the Historic Columbia River Highway is the more scenic choice. Of course, seeing the falls goes without saying. Beyond

that, Angel's Lookout is well worth the trek, and Rooster Rock State Park boasts a nude beach for those who feel inclined to get down and dirty with the elements. Finish up with some home-cooked goods from Corbett Country Market before heading downstream to the Columbia River Gorge.

To get there, cross over the Bridge of the Gods into Washington State and follow the riverbank eastward. Bigfoot Coffee Roasters in Stevenson is a great pit stop en route; you'll need the energy for what's ahead. Namely, an awesome hike up to the Dog Mountain Lookout, where you'll get a panoramic goat's-eye view of the gorge. The further east you continue on the Lewis and Clark Highway, the deeper you get into Columbia Gorge Wine Country. Plan your accommodations accordingly and ask around →

You could spend a week here and never get bored. The peaks, the hikes, the lakes, the wildlife—all of it is breathtaking.

The area surrounding Mount Rainier is home to unparalleled hiking and camping. Especially awe-inspiring is the Skyline Trail, which loops 6 miles (10 kilometers) around a little place called Paradise. Reward your climb to 7,051 feet (2,149 meters) with a dip in a lake closer to sea level.

→ to see which vineyard locals recommend. The Society Hotel in Bingen is a great place to spend the night, and you'll find no shortage of delectable dining across the bridge in the city of Hood River.

Fuel up both car and crew—at the homely Carmen's Kitchen, perhaps—the next morning, as you'll hit the road for around 200 miles (322 kilometers) en route to Mount Rainier National Park. You'll find a great lunch stopover at the Trout Lake Country Inn, which you can follow up with some fresh air at the Trout Creek Meadow. From there, you'll have an unobstructed view of Mount Adams, Washington's second-highest peak, and, you guessed it, another maybe-active volcano. The hikes to Luna Lake and Island Lake at the mountain's base are astonishing. If you find the area simply too beautiful to rush through,

consider pitching a tent at the nearby Twin Falls Campground. Otherwise, continue north on Forest Road 23 until you get within striking distance of Mount Rainier, a confirmed active volcano. The Stormking Cabins & Spa offer an exceptional sleepover.

Mount Rainier National Park is quintessential PNW. You could spend a week here and never get bored. The peaks, the hikes, the lakes, the wildlife—all of it is breathtaking. Don't be surprised if coming here leads to an impromptu prolonging of the trip. If you opt to keep things moving, the curvy Stevens Canyon Road will lead you deep into nature and to the base of dozens of trailheads should you want to go deeper. Take it all in because it's off to the concrete jungle after this.

Seattle, of course, needs a full book for itself. But we'll say this: don't skip the chowder at Pike Place Market. Alternatively, try some French-Vietnamese fusion fare at Stateside or ask some locals where to find the city's best sushi. As for accommodation, the Ace Hotel is a Belltown gem that'll take you back to Seattle's maritime roots. Perhaps best of all, though, is that the majestic North Cascades and Olympic national parks are just a short drive away. Just in case you couldn't wait to get back on the road and into the great outdoors. ◆

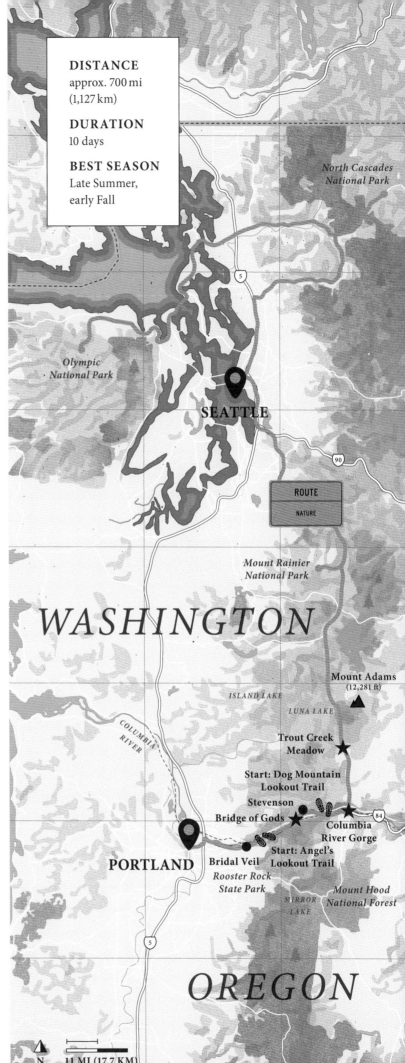

DISTANCE
approx. 700 mi
(1,127 km)

DURATION
10 days

BEST SEASON
Late Summer,
early Fall

North Cascades
National Park

Olympic
National Park

SEATTLE

ROUTE

NATURE

Mount Rainier
National Park

WASHINGTON

Mount Adams
(12,281 ft)

ISLAND LAKE

LUNA LAKE

COLUMBIA
RIVER

Trout Creek
Meadow

Start: Dog Mountain
Lookout Trail

Stevenson

Bridge of Gods

Columbia
River Gorge

PORTLAND

Bridal Veil

Start: Angel's
Lookout Trail

Rooster Rock
State Park

*MIRROR
LAKE*

Mount Hood
National Forest

OREGON

N

11 MI (17.7 KM)

Travel Back in Time with a Thrilling Adventure on the Historic Oregon Trail

BUFFALO, NEW YORK → OREGON CITY, OREGON

This odyssey traces the historic westward wagon routes of America's early settlers.

There was a time when nobody knew what lay west of the Missouri River except for the Indigenous populations. To uncover the mysteries of the frontier, President Thomas Jefferson sent Meriwether Lewis and William Clark on their now-famous expedition in 1804. The explorers reached the Pacific Ocean and returned with stories of untamed lands and untouched nature.

Shortly after, fur traders laid out the Oregon Trail, a 2,100-mile (3,380-kilometer) route starting in Independence, Missouri, and ending in Oregon City, Oregon. As the trail's passability improved, the first wagon trains set out in 1836. Throughout the 1840s, '50s, and '60s, nearly 500,000 settlers, ranchers, farmers, and miners made the treacherous journey west, enduring hardship, illness, even death.

Designated a national historic trail, today what's left of the Oregon Trail carves through remote countryside and passes by historical landmarks. This 3,325-mile (5,351-kilometer), four-week, summer trip kicks off east of the Trail's origin point to pack in more sights and more adventure. You'll begin in Buffalo, New York, go west to Missouri where the trail officially starts, and follow it to Oregon.

To honor the historic-route theme of this trip, visit the launch of another famous trail: Route 66.

In Buffalo, visit the city's most popular attraction, Niagara Falls. Three falls actually make up what we call Niagara Falls: the mighty American Falls on the U.S. side, the rounded Horseshoe Falls on the Canadian side, and the ethereal Bridal Veil Falls.

Also on the U.S.-Canada border, you'll find another impressive body of water. The fourth-largest of North America's Great Lakes, Lake Erie sprawls as wide as an ocean. As you drive to Cleveland, Ohio, look north through the trees to spot the slate-blue waves. Close-up views are best enjoyed at the Cleveland Lakefront Nature Preserve or Edgewater Beach Park.

Continue west, a picturesque drive through the heart of Indiana Amish Country.

What used to be one of America's most treacherous trails is now a paved paradise. Covering 2,100 miles (3,380 kilometers) with tire tracks in six states, the Oregon Trail hearkens back to the age of westward expansion. The wooden wagons may be gone, but the sense of wonder remains.

This rural region invites you to slow down and enjoy the simple things in life. A home-cooked meal. A horse-and-buggy ride. Shopping for handmade goods at a flea market. No matter what you do, be sure to stop by Menno-Hof, a museum that offers thoughtful insights into the Amish community.

As you near the bright lights of Chicago, Illinois, detour to Indiana Dunes National Park. Its roots date to the 1900s when nature enthusiasts fought to preserve the sand dunes that tower 200 feet (61 meters) high and have taken thousands of years to form. Scout for rare birds as you walk the park's edge along Lake Michigan (the second-largest of the Great Lakes).

Chicago also abuts Lake Michigan, with its skyscrapers lining the shore. Check into The Hoxton Hotel in the hip West Loop neighborhood before boarding a boat for the 90-minute Chicago River Architecture Tour. Not only do the guides share fascinating tidbits on the Windy City's structural feats, they also inform you about history.

When you disembark, hit up one of Chicago's great museums, such as the Museum of Science and Industry or the Field Museum. To honor the historic-route theme of this trip, visit the launch of another famous trail: Route 66. The Mother Road, which runs from Chicago to Santa Monica, begins at the Art Institute of Chicago. Leave the city to grab lunch in quaint Galena, Illinois. Nestled on the Galena River and famous for its well-preserved 19th-century buildings, this pretty-as-a-postcard place oozes charm.

Across the state line in Iowa, check out Cedar Rock State Park, home to the Frank Lloyd Wright-designed estate of Agnes and Lowell Walter. Then head over to the Field of Dreams Movie Site, a celebration of all things baseball, and, of course, the adored 1989 film of the same name.

In Sioux City, pay homage to a member of the Lewis and Clark expedition at Sergeant Floyd Monument. It's the burial site of Sergeant Charles Floyd, Jr., the only member of the Corps of Discovery to die on the trek; he succumbed to a ruptured appendix.

Independence, Missouri, is your chance to stand where Oregon Trail pioneers geared up for their sojourn west. See historic landmarks like Independence Courthouse Square, →

Who says you have to keep on the trail? Wind down with a leisurely soak at the Mountain Village Resort's natural hot spring or take a detour along roads less traveled. There's plenty to discover for wide eyes and open minds.

→ the plaque marking the start of the trail, and the National Frontier Trails Museum.

Cross into Kansas to Alcove Spring, a favorite stop for Oregon Trail travelers thanks to a natural spring and waterfall. An easy hike parallels wagon swales, deep depressions in the earth made from thousands of wagons. Before you reach Nebraska, take pictures of the Hollenberg Pony Express Station State Historic Site in Hanover, Kansas. Built in 1858, it's the most intact Pony Express stop in the United States.

As the open landscape of Nebraska welcomes you, settle in at Scottsbluff. Find cozy lodging at Barn Anew Bed and Breakfast or more rustic accommodations at Riverside Campground. This will be your base for exploring Scotts Bluff National Monument. Must-dos

at this 3,000-acre (1,214-hectare) landmark include seeing the interactive exhibits dedicated to the Oregon Trail, driving the Summit Road, and hiking the prairie trails.

This rural region invites you to slow down and enjoy the simple things in life.

Before continuing west, consider a 3.5-hour detour north to South Dakota's famed Mount Rushmore. The colossal granite rock formations sport the carved-in-stone faces of four

U. S. presidents: George Washington, Thomas Jefferson, Theodore Roosevelt, and Abraham Lincoln. Early designs called for the inclusion of Lewis and Clark and their guide Sacagawea, Buffalo Bill Cody, and Lakota war leader Crazy Horse. Though none of these made it onto the monument, Crazy Horse does have an under-construction memorial nearby, which will be the largest mountain sculpture in the world when—if ever—completed.

Return to the Oregon Trail and motor west to Wyoming's Guernsey Ruts. These are some of the best wagon runs along the trail, measuring 4 feet (1.2 meters) deep. Pair this visit with a trip to Register Cliff Historic Site in Guernsey. Weary travelers spent the night here and many of them inscribed their names →

Consider a detour north to Mount Rushmore. The colossal granite rock formations sport the carved-in-stone faces of four U.S. presidents.

Yellowstone is where the bison roam—and often cause traffic jams. Just as common and no less eye-catching are the park's active geysers and more than 10,000 hot springs and other geothermal features, many of which are connected by the Grand Loop Road.

→ into the limestone rock. Today's visitors can see these names, some from 1820s-era fur traders and trappers, but most from Oregon Trail settlers passing through in the 1840s and '50s.

It's one thing to walk the ruts—it's another to rumble along the pitted earth in an actual covered wagon. To experience first-hand what the Oregon Trail trekkers did, stop in Casper, Wyoming, for a two-hour wagon tour with Historic Trails West.

Once you're comfortably settled back in your modern mode of transportation, take another side trip, this time to the country's first national park, Yellowstone. There's nothing like this wondrous place where geysers erupt, springs run hot, scalding ash petrifies trees, and the entire park sits on a massive volcanic caldera.

See more evidence of volcanic activity at Craters of the Moon National Monument in Arco, Idaho. So named for its basalt terrain dotted with cinder cones and striped with lava flows, the monument invites you to hike miles of wilderness trails (you can even camp) or drive a 7-mile (11-kilometer) scenic loop.

Each bend in this road is more scenic than the last.

Onward to Boise, Idaho, for an overnight layover. Spend time in the city's Basque Block, the largest Basque community outside of Spain.

Soak up the culture at the Basque Center, stroll the Basque Market, or nosh on traditional Basque cuisine. For more Oregon Trail history, head to the Idaho State Museum or check out the Old Idaho Penitentiary, a prison that once housed more than 13,000 people, from train robbers and desperadoes to bounty hunters and bandits.

Your last stop in Idaho should be Fort Boise, a replica of the 1834 original that served as a supply stop for those heading west on the Oregon Trail. Once you reach Oregon, go to the National Historic Oregon Trail Interpretive Center in Baker City. Artifacts, life-sized dioramas, true stories of pioneers, plus wagon ruts and remnants of a gold mine all illustrate the struggles of the settlers. →

Though your drive
will prove far less dangerous
than that of the
early pioneers, it'll be no less
infused with promise,
excitement, and surprises.

The Oregon Trail is pure #vanlife, but that doesn't mean you should skip a stopover in the Windy City. After a few days in Chicago's urban jungle, you'll be pining for a return to the open road and all its charms.

→ As you make your way to Oregon City, hop on the Historic Columbia River Highway for a looping drive above the river gorge. Each bend in the road is more scenic than the last. As the Columbia River twists and turns, waterfalls plunge seemingly out of nowhere. In Hood River, see the 635-foot (194-meter) Multnomah Falls from the iconic Benson Bridge.

Oregon City might live in the shadow of trendy Portland (an optional detour if for nothing else than cult-favorite Voodoo Doughnuts), but it boasts two important honors. It was Oregon's first state capital, and it concludes the epic Oregon Trail. It was here, where the Willamette River meets the waters of the Columbia, that weary travelers arrived after months of pilgrimage. Those who survived the expedition rested and

refueled, then went about scouting for a new patch of land to claim and call home. The End of the Trail Interpretive Center offers an in-depth overview of what awaited the wagoneers in Oregon.

In Oregon City, the weary travelers arrived after months of pilgrimage.

It could be said that those who crossed the Oregon Trail were the original road trippers—of course with covered wagons instead of cars. These daring travelers left the homes they knew

and embarked on a course filled with danger, hope, and possibility. Though your drive will prove far less treacherous than that of the early pioneers, it'll be no less infused with promise, excitement, and surprises. That's what road trips are made for, right? ◆

DISTANCE
approx. 3,325 mi
(5,351 km)

DURATION
4 weeks

BEST SEASON
Summer

Washington

USA

Montana

Multnomah Falls

OREGON CITY

Idaho

*Yellowstone
National Park*

National Historic
Oregon Trail
Interpretive Center

Craters of the Moon
National Monument

Mount Rushm
(5,725 ft)

Oregon

Boise

Wyoming

Casper

Register Cliff
Historic Site

Scotts Bluff
National Monument

Salt Lake City

Denver

Nevada

Sacramento

Colorado

California

Arizona

New Mexico

MEXICO

N

56 MI (90.1 KM)

Explore New Worlds without Ever Having to Leave This One

SALT LAKE CITY, UTAH → BRYCE CANYON, UTAH

The "Mighty Five" national parks south of Salt Lake City deliver inspirational, otherworldly landscapes.

The fact that there has been human life in this part of the world for some 12,000 years should speak to how alluring and inspirational the region is. The rocky expanse of Southern Utah was home to the very first Paleo-Americans in the earliest days of civilization. In time, the caves and cliffs became the foundations for the dwellings built by the Ancestral Puebloans, and eventually, the Mormons arrived in the mid-19th century, taming this harsh environment even further.

Salt Lake City is now a modern, sophisticated city, but the regions that lie beyond—now designated national parks—still have something of those primordial times about them. Ancient rock formations—hundreds of millions of years old—have created otherworldly landscapes, and exploring them often feels like you're walking on the surface of another planet. Little wonder that the five major national parks south of Salt Lake City welcome around four million visitors a year between them. Feel free to take a worthwhile detour to Monument Valley as well.

From Salt Lake City, drive about four hours southeast to reach Arches National Park. Aptly named, the park boasts a record number of natural stone arches within its limits. No other place on Earth comes close to these 2,000 dramatic formations, perfectly balanced and creating huge stone rainbows against the endless desert skies. These incredible structures took millions of years to form, and far into the future, they will eventually collapse. For now, they stand boldly, with famous landmarks such as Turret Arch and Delicate Arch seeming almost too perfect to have been shaped naturally. The geological eons of the Earth's existence are etched into the visible layers, shades of red and orange telling stories of huge environmental shifts and epoch-defining events.

Visitors can hike any of the many trails, of course, but there's also a popular scenic drive, which hits the major viewing spots and takes around three hours, allowing for 10 minutes of wonderment at each natural amphitheater. Balanced Rock has a very easily accessible loop that children and wheelchair users can navigate. Mountain bikes are available for rental in Moab, and experienced rock climbers flock to the park for both the challenging overhangs and the idyllic backdrop.

From Arches National Park, it is about a 45-minute drive on UT-313W to Canyonlands National Park. Prehistoric geological processes have created a scenic masterpiece in this park.

There's something extraterrestrial about driving between the mesas of Canyonlands National Park. Writing about the park, the American author Edward Abbey once called it "the most weird, wonderful, magical place on earth." Probably because there's truly nothing else like it on our planet.

Primordial rivers—the Colorado and Green Rivers—carved out the pathways that we see now. The resulting formations are wonderfully diverse, with canyons, spires, mesas, and buttes as far as the eye can see.

Canyonlands is divided into distinct districts known as the Needles, the Maze, and a green mountain plateau called Island in the Sky. This park feels much more remote, the districts some four or five hours apart by car, and as there are no direct linking roads, many people choose one district per visit.

The most popular is, as you might guess, Island in the Sky, and for reasons beyond its easier accessibility. Standing at Mesa Arch as the sun rises (or sets) provides a view of the pillars and valleys that could be Martian, just glowing, barren rock stretching to the horizon. The Needles has its own draws, with hundreds of colorful sandstone towers, while the Maze is a destination for more experienced hikers, with its stark, rugged terrain and intertwining channels.

Heading west for a couple of hours, the desiccated rock slowly gives way to greenery again as you approach the entrance of Capitol Reef National Park. This is still very much the heart of Red Rock Country, but at least some vegetation seems to thrive here. The park is partly named for the Capitol Building, thanks to early prospectors. At the turn of the 20th century, they arrived to be confronted with the white domes of Waterpocket Fold, reminding them of the Washington D.C. landmark. →

No other place on Earth
comes close to these
2,000 dramatic formations,
perfectly balanced
and creating huge
stone rainbows against the
endless desert skies.

Zion National Park, Bryce Canyon National Park, Capitol Reef National Park, Canyonlands National Park, Arches National Park—Utah really is spoiled for choice. Where else can you visit five national parks in a single day? (Not that you should.)

→ Other visitors have likened the panorama to a tropical reef, such are the many changing colors that appear and beguile onlookers as the sun changes position. Capitol Gorge leads to the glorious white Capitol Dome, and close by another famous structure, the towering red plinth of Chimney Rock, reaches up 300 feet (91 meters) against the blue sky. At Capitol Gorge, look for the art of the Fremont Culture, who daubed and etched into the rocks between 300 CE and 1300 CE, their creative legacy still visible today.

Next, it's off to the most famous of the Mighty Five, Zion National Park, around three and a half hours southwest of Capitol Reef. The 2,000-foot (610-meter) rock walls that were created by the ancient Virgin River are now a highlight for hikers—reds, pinks, and orange

tones creating a multicolored playground. The park's name means "refuge," and thanks to early Mormon settlers, many of the park's regions have a religious theme to their names.

You'll notice the increase in tree life here, with willow and cottonwood oaks lining some of the trails around the lower foothills, and the park is home to over 1,000 species of flora. Deer and bobcats live here, and the foliage reaches luxuriant levels in some places. The infrastructure is well established, and there's a free shuttle service that runs from the visitors' center and stops at nine locations around the park.

There are dozens of well-maintained hiking trails for adventurers of all abilities, from the 1.3-mile (2.1-kilometer) paved River Walk to multiday expeditions along less forgiving paths.

Geological highlights include the Great White Throne, Court of the Patriarchs, Angels Landing, and Weeping Rock. For a real feeling of remote exploration, a separate entrance leads to the Kolob Canyons with a panorama that rewards the extra effort involved.

From Zion National Park, it's about a two-hour drive northeast to the last of the Mighty Five—Bryce Canyon National Park. As you approach, you'll begin to see the park's famous pinnacle rock formations (known as hoodoos), which give off a fiery glow in the sun. There are more of these striking, nature-sculpted peaks here than anywhere else on the globe.

The park's name is a little deceiving, and the "canyon" here is in reality a series of cavernous natural amphitheaters. Standing at Inspiration

Point at dawn, you can become enchanted by the army of hundreds of orange, pink, and red hoodoos that line up around the rocky recess of the Bryce Amphitheater. Explore the park on foot, meandering through the labyrinthine trails, threading between the pillars through channels carved by the elements so many millennia ago.

Except for winter, there's no bad time to head into these national parks, each season putting on a different but equally stunning display of color and landscape. It's hard to believe that these formations and their endless nuances of shade and color just happen naturally on this planet. You can believe the evidence of your own eyes as you put your hands on the millennia-old rock and appreciate the splendor, just as our ancestors did some 12,000 years ago. ◆

DISTANCE
approx. 692 mi
(1,114 km)

DURATION
1 week

BEST SEASON
Spring, Summer,
Fall

UTAH

SALT LAKE CITY

ROUTE
NATIONAL
PARKS

Arches
National
Park

Moab

GREEN RIVER

Canyonlands
National Park

COLORADO RIVER

Capitol Reef
National Park

Bryce
Canyon
National
Park

Zion
National
Park

Kolob Canyons

Monument
Valley

12 MI (19.3 KM)

Hightail It to the Desert: From the City to Picturesque Solitude

LOS ANGELES, CALIFORNIA → LAS VEGAS, NEVADA

The buzzing metropolis of Los Angeles gives way
to the brutal beauty of Death Valley.

It's hard to imagine a more stark contrast than the one between the neon-lit cityscape of metropolitan Los Angeles and the barren, scorching salt flats of Death Valley National Park. This pilgrimage is one of extremes, from perhaps the coolest city in the world to the hottest place on Earth and the driest place in North America.

Even within an hour on the road, there's some heavy foreshadowing of the stark changes that lie ahead. As you nudge out past the sprawling L. A. suburbs and beyond Santa Clarita and Palmdale, CA-14N heads into more rural climes. Cinephiles may want to divert around Lancaster to the near-ghost town of Hi Vista. Here you can take a peek at Twin Pines Chapel, a famous location in Quentin Tarantino's movie *Kill Bill*.

This pilgrimage is one of extremes, from the coolest city to the hottest place on Earth.

A sign of the brutal but beautiful desert to come emerges at Vasquez Rocks Natural Area Park and Nature Center. Tilted sandstone formations rise out of the sands like the fins of huge subterranean beasts, the strata of eons of evolution visible to all. They glow crimson and gold in the sun as it moves across the huge open skies.

Traveling north and then northwest from the city of Mojave, you'll push even further into the Californian wilderness. As you do, the landscape's levels of otherworldliness start to become even more noticeable. You'll feel like you're on a lunar safari as you pass the Trona Pinnacles, calcium carbonate spires that were formed between 10,000 and 100,000 years ago. At this point, you're actually traversing an ancient lake bed, and it's easy to imagine this as a hidden, subaquatic world.

Before you descend into the full furnace of Death Valley, the relatively lush vegetation of Sequoia National Park and the foothills of Mount Whitney offer a last reprieve. Keep an eye out for sand food, strange vegetation that grows in this part of the world, and which looks like a land-based jellyfish or anemone. Take in the multicolored splendor of the Alabama Hills, which rose from unfathomably violent eruptions some 100 million years ago, and which now provide →

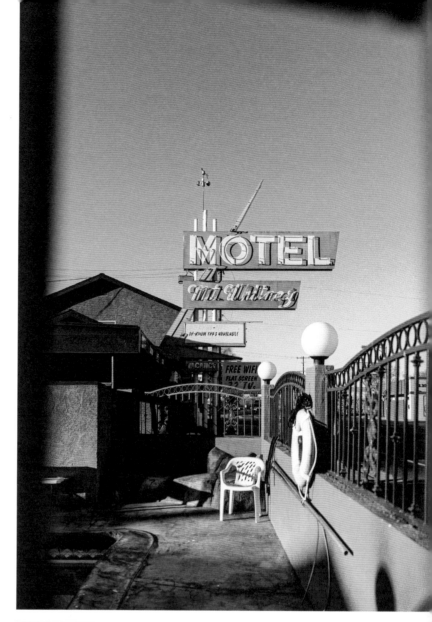

Before you descend
into the full furnace of
Death Valley, the relatively
lush vegetation of
Sequoia National Park
and the foothills
of Mount Whitney offer
a last reprieve.

Last chance to stock up on booze. From here on out, everything's completely dry—and excruciatingly hot. In fact, the world's hottest temperature, 134 °F (57 °C), was recorded in 1911 at aptly named Furnace Creek in Death Valley.

→ a kaleidoscope of glowing shades thanks to their complex geology.

Driving along the snaking, increasingly desiccated CA-190E, you'll take around two hours to reach Death Valley National Park. The place-names that you pass really underline the ominous nature of this region: Stovepipe Wells, Furnace Creek, and in the background, the Funeral Mountains. Death Valley is a vast expanse, and some 3.4 million acres (1.4 million hectares) make up this park, the largest of its kind in the Lower 48.

It's a surprisingly diverse environment, with everything from stark salt flats to idyllic water-fed canyons, from basins that sit below sea level to peaks that reach 11,000 feet (3,353 meters) into the sky.

A network of 1,000 miles (1,609 kilometers) of roads (paved and dirt) provides for extensive exploration. A word about safety: bring more water than you think you might need, as it's very easy to dehydrate. Avoid very remote spots, especially if you're alone or you're unfamiliar with the area, and make sure that you have plenty of gas and that your car's water tank is topped off.

The submarine-like world first glimpsed at the Trona Pinnacles becomes even more vivid here. The Mesquite Flat Sand Dunes rise up from the ground in wave-like formations, seas of sand that glint with their ever-shifting hues. It's a majestic sight that attracts photographers from around the world, and even exploring just a little beyond the parking lot here will envelop you in a comforting blanket of solitude.

One place to survey the scorched panorama is from Zabriskie Point, just beyond Furnace Creek. From here, the sun-baked slopes stretch out before you, almost devoid of all vegetation. Deep gullies are etched into the hills, a result of the dramatically heavy but rare rainfalls that happen every now and then. This erodes the sandstone, reshaping the landscape in an endless dance.

As well as having the driest stretches of North America, Death Valley is also home to the lowest of the low: Badwater Basin. These infamous salt flats reside at a depth of 282 feet (86 meters) below sea level, a fact made all the more apparent by the looming mountains that surround this natural wonder. Small pools of water exist here, but their salt content is so high →

Contrary to its name, Death Valley is actually home to plenty of life. Small amounts of rain can result in bursts of wildflowers, and the roots of many desert plants can reach up to 59 feet (18 meters) into the ground for water. You may even stumble upon birds, reptiles, and mammals like jackrabbits, coyotes, and sheep.

→ that no life could thrive within them. The salt appears as snow, breaking into crystals as you walk along the crusty flats.

Again, you may feel very far removed from everyday reality. Scenery like this—brutally formed and unrelenting in its extremity—is rare, and its disregard for sustaining life makes us feel somehow more alive. Some 5,500 feet (1,676 meters) above Badwater Basin, on the ridge of the Black Mountains, Dante's View is a figurative throne from which to survey this astonishing kingdom.

All of the park's features, from the lowest flats to the highest peaks, are visible from here. Dark specks—fellow travelers—edge across white plains or along mountain ridges in the distance. Come for sunrise or sunset for a near-spiritual experience. Although it is one of the most popular spots in the whole park, there is space enough to find tranquility and to feel as alone as you'd like to be. Don't forget that the entire park is designated an International Dark Sky Park, and so stargazing is truly phenomenal here.

Onward into the depths of the park, and the Dumont Dunes undulate for miles and miles, surrounded by steep volcanic hills. This region is a huge draw for off-road driving, but even if you didn't bring your own ATV, you can appreciate the curves and patterns of the sands. There are excellent camping opportunities here, and again, the night sky is a thing of wonder, the Milky Way and its mysteries laid out as you gaze upwards.

By now you may be feeling the itch to return to more urban surroundings, despite the incredible natural variations of the park. Los Angeles is around four hours from here if you want to make a closed loop, but for variation, within two hours you can be in downtown Las Vegas. After a time spent doing nothing but regarding the natural world, a slice of ridiculous artifice might be just what you need, and the ersatz Eiffel Tower and pyramids together with endless neon and buzz may be a refuge in themselves. ◆

There are excellent camping opportunities here, and again, the night sky is a thing of wonder, the Milky Way and its mysteries laid out as you gaze upwards.

NEVADA

DISTANCE
approx. 650 mi
(1,046 km)

DURATION
1 week

BEST SEASON
Spring

395

95

Mesquite Flat Sand Dunes

Mount Whitney
(14,505 ft)

Death Valley
National Park

190

Zabriskie Point

ROUTE
ROCK
CLIMBING

Badwater Basin

LAS VEGAS

Dumont Dunes

Trona Pinnacles

127

15

Mojave

14

40

Hi Vista

15

Vasquez Rocks
Natural Area Park

Palmdale

CALIFORNIA

Santa Clarita

LOS ANGELES

10

8 MI (12.9 KM)

Skirt the Ocean: Soak In the Views on This Pacific Coast Highway Trip

SAN DIEGO, CALIFORNIA → VANCOUVER, BRITISH COLUMBIA, CANADA

As one of the most famous drives in the United States,
this storied highway showcases the best of the West Coast.

R eady for vistas galore? This 1,500-mile (2,414-kilometer) road trip gives you ocean view after ocean view. If you think that might get boring after two weeks, think again. The Pacific Coast Highway (officially Interstate Highway 1, more colloquially, the PCH) is the only way to immerse yourself in the shape-shifting geography of the West Coast. The road clings to the shoreline from its southernmost point in San Diego to its terminus in Northern California. There it merges with U.S. Highway 101, a connector to Vancouver. Along the way, seaside villages neighbor big cities, drawing a constellation of places knitted together by a giant body of water. Watch as the scenery transforms from sun-drenched sand to bustling harbors to windswept cliffs and then from craggy beaches to secluded coves and lighthouse-studded overlooks. Go slow and stop often.

Grab takeout, then spend the afternoon at one of L. A.'s palm-lined beaches.

Plan for a summer sojourn, an ideal season for this drive. It's also a perfect time to be in San Diego, your starting point and home to the most beautiful beaches in the world. From your accommodations at the historic Hotel del Coronado, you're steps from sun, sand, and surf. The hotel—featured in Marilyn Monroe's 1958 film *Some Like It Hot*—cozies up to Coronado Beach with its glittering sand. (Literally. The mineral mica in the grains sparkles in the light). In nearby La Jolla, Black's Beach treats you to quiet seclusion, and La Jolla Shores offers a sandy stretch popular with families.

When you've had your fill of beach fun, visit the Birch Aquarium, the largest oceanographic museum in the United States, or Cabrillo National Monument, which sits at the highest point in San Diego and grants breathtaking views of the city.

Follow the Pacific north to Los Angeles. Here, your home away from home is inland at The LINE LA, a boutique hotel in Koreatown. This vibrant area has plenty of great eats—Korean markets, restaurants, and food trucks—but a few miles north in a modest strip mall, you'll discover unforgettable Thai food at Jitlada. Grab takeout, then spend the afternoon at one of L. A.'s

Cruising the Pacific Coast Highway is every road-tripper's dream. Bring it to life by loading up your SUV and hitting the road for a couple weeks in early or late summer. Whether under the stars, the redwoods, or your vehicle's roof, you'll never get bored of the sleeping options.

palm-lined beaches: Huntington, Santa Monica, Venice, or Point Dume in Malibu.

The PCH inches north, leaving the crowds of Southern California behind to enter the vineyard-covered hills of Santa Barbara. To sample the region's vino without venturing off course, park yourself downtown. More than 30 tasting rooms comprise the Santa Barbara Urban Wine Trail.

After a well-rested night, follow the PCH to San Simeon. With its unspoiled beaches and rugged coastline, it's easy to see why William Randolph Hearst chose this location for his dream home. The stately Hearst Castle is more than just a house, though; it's an architectural showpiece and an accredited museum. After a tour, relax at Hearst Memorial Beach or visit

Piedras Blancas Light Station, an 1875 lighthouse still in operation today.

The staggering seascapes of Big Sur envelop you on the meandering drive north. This section of road was built starting in 1919 and was the first leg of the PCH to open. While you'll find no shortage of inviting hotels in Big Sur, there are few experiences that rival that of falling asleep to the sight of the stars above and the sound of the surf below. Book a campsite at Pfeiffer Burns State Park, where the ocean meets a waterfall and granite cliffs rise from a rocky beach. The next day, take in breakfast on the terrace of The Sur House, then head north to Carmel-by-the-Sea.

It seems as if all roads lead to the water in Carmel. Feel like an ocean-loving local by visiting Point Lobos State Natural Reserve—popular →

A copy of Jack Kerouac's *On the Road* is sure to get you in the Pacific Coast spirit and makes for a great companion on the shores of Big Sur or patios of Los Angeles. Who knows, maybe you'll be inspired to write your own Great American Novel.

→ with birdwatchers—or Carmel Beach, a long crescent of sand where dogs are free to roam off-leash. Carmel has several interesting claims to fame, one being that Clint Eastwood was the mayor from 1986 to 1988.

On the way to San Francisco, a 2.5-hour drive north on the PCH, you'll pass by the sleepy seaside towns of Santa Cruz and Half Moon Bay. Once in San Francisco, the pace of life kicks up a notch. No visit is complete without a tour of the historic, prison-on-an-island Alcatraz, nor should you miss noshing among the food stalls at the Ferry Building or visiting the museums and gardens at Golden Gate Park.

Other bucket-list items: samusa soup at Burma Superstar, a cable car ride, and City Lights Bookstore, once a meeting place for 1950s Beat writers like Allen Ginsberg and Jack Kerouac. Before departing San Fran, spare a day for a Sonoma detour to join an action-packed bike, balloon, and brew tour with Up & Away Ballooning.

Though you can use U.S. Highway 101 to shortcut the trip to your next destination of Avenue of the Giants, stay on Interstate Highway 1. It's a longer zigzag up the coast, but it's prettier and it delivers you to lovely little places such as Bodega Bay (where Alfred Hitchcock filmed *The Birds*) and Mendocino.

In Leggett, the PCH merges with US-101 and you'll soon be at Avenue of the Giants, a 31-mile (50-kilometer) adventure through statuesque redwoods—the tallest trees on Earth. See more of them, plus oak woodlands, prairies, and rivers at Redwood National Park in Orick.

Also in Orick is Gold Bluffs Beach, a secret spot for beachcombers. Fun fact: Stephen Spielberg filmed scenes at nearby Fern Canyon Trail for *Jurassic Park 2*.

Crescent City is the final stop in California, and it's the proverbial fork in the road if you choose to go northeast to Crater Lake National Park. This six-hour round-trip detour rewards you with a peek at a sapphire-blue lake formed by a volcano that erupted and collapsed 7,700 years ago. With a maximum depth of 1,950 feet (594 m), it is one of the deepest in the world.

If you skip Crater Lake, continue on U.S. Highway 101 up the coast into Oregon and to the fishing and crabbing community of Gold Beach, named after the shore where miners once found gold. →

Mere miles separate the lush greens of Humboldt Redwoods State Park from the Pacific's crashing coastline. You'll find plenty of campsites where you can pitch a tent—just make sure to book in advance, as you won't be the only one looking to lay your head under the redwoods.

→ You're a long way from the board-walk piers and surf cities of Southern California on this jagged-edged stretch of the Pacific Coast. Boulders and bluffs mark the way and lighthouses blink atop cliffs. Pay a visit to a few of these, such as Cape Blanco Lighthouse in Bandon and Heceta Head Lighthouse near Florence. On a 1,000-foot- (305-meter-) high perch, Heceta is one of the most photographed lighthouses in the United States.

As you follow the Oregon shoreline, train your gaze on the water to spot migrating whales. The Three Capes Scenic Route of Cape Meares, Cape Kiwanda, and Cape Lookout offers vantage points at which to see these enormous creatures.

View more wildlife at Cannon Beach. The tufted puffin seabirds make their home from April to July on the beach's iconic formation, Haystack Rock. Snap photos and then relish a hyper-local dinner of fresh oysters, just-caught salmon, and wild mushrooms at Wayfarer Restaurant.

Drift east from the coast for the next two locales: Portland and Seattle.

Downtown Portland is highly walkable, so stay at the centrally located Ace Hotel. It serves the city's famous Stumptown Coffee. Grab a cup to go and stroll Pioneer Courthouse Square and the South Park Blocks, which lead to the Portland Art Museum and the Portland Farmers Market.

Before dinner at Screen Door (a comfort-food restaurant), appreciate why Portland is known as the Rose City. At the Portland Rose Garden, 10,000 roses bloom among the lush lawns.

Three hours and about 100,000 people separate Portland and Seattle, but the cities share a mutual love for fresh food and the outdoors. In Seattle, these come together at Matt's in The Market, a restaurant with views of Elliott Bay and a menu of local scallops, King salmon, sturgeon, and oysters.

Thanks to nearly 500 parks throughout the city, you can join joggers and walkers at green spaces like Discovery Park and Seward Park. And to glimpse Seattle's oddball side, check out the public-art sculpture, the Fremont Troll.

Scoot north, threading the waterways of northwest Washington to Vancouver, British Columbia. This Canadian city is an inter-national mecca for artists, musicians, and film-makers. Book a room at the EXchange Hotel;

situated downtown, the hotel's location makes it easy to take in the city's thriving scene, from shopping Robson Street and seeing a live theater performance to dining at hotspots like Forage and Bao Bei.

It took 15 years for the Pacific Coast Highway to be constructed in the 1920s and '30s. Since then, it's become one of the most beloved and fabled roads in America, a ribbon of blacktop unspooling over landscapes as dramatic and splendid as they are diverse. A road trip on the PCH is one you won't soon forget. The sight of fog lifting its veil to reveal the pounding surf, the seagulls' call, the smell of salt air, and that feel of the wind whipping your hair through the open car window—these are memories that will stay with you for a lifetime. ◆

Three hours and about
100,000 people
separate Portland and
Seattle, Washington,
but the cities share a
mutual love for fresh food
and the outdoors.

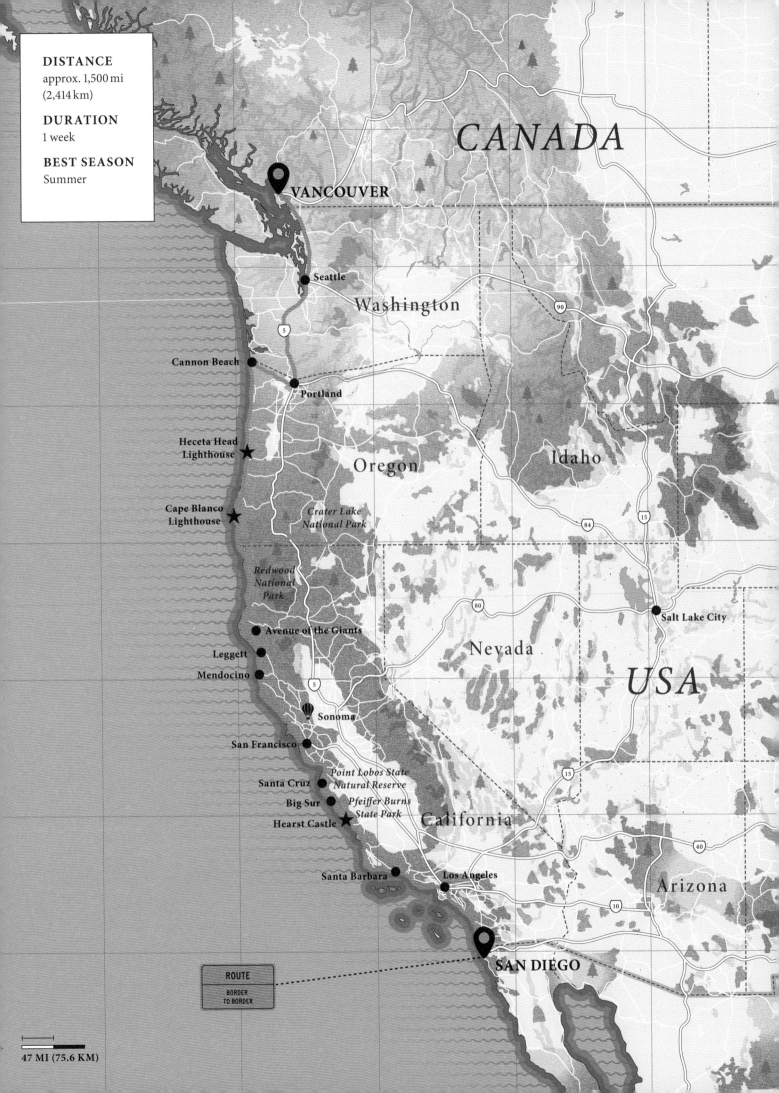

DISTANCE
approx. 1,500 mi
(2,414 km)

DURATION
1 week

BEST SEASON
Summer

CANADA

VANCOUVER

Seattle

Washington

Cannon Beach

Portland

Heceta Head
Lighthouse

Oregon

Idaho

Crater Lake
National Park

Redwood
National
Park

Cape Blanco
Lighthouse

Salt Lake City

Avenue of the Giants

Leggett

Mendocino

Nevada

USA

Sonoma

San Francisco

Santa Cruz

Point Lobos State
Natural Reserve

Big Sur

Pfeiffer Burns
State Park

Hearst Castle

California

Arizona

Santa Barbara

Los Angeles

SAN DIEGO

ROUTE

BORDER
TO BORDER

47 MI (75.6 KM)

Embark On an Expedition through California's Natural Landscapes

SAN FRANCISCO, CALIFORNIA

This epic journey is what bucket lists are made of, from scenic coastal drives to famous national parks.

California possesses an allure unlike any other place. The sun seems to shine a little brighter, the skies beam a little bluer. Though its city centers like Los Angeles and San Francisco are known the world over as thriving cultural hubs, it is the state's wild beauty that inspires songs, movies, even entire books. And these natural lands are vast and ripe for exploration. Case in point: there are more national parks in California than in any other state.

This 10-day, 930-mile (1,497-kilometer) trip begins and concludes in San Francisco. Along the way, you will wind through the Golden State's most stunning scenery. A forest of giant sequoias. The calm waters of Monterey Bay. Big Sur's coastal vistas and Yosemite's rugged rock formations. As you take to the open road, don't resist California's siren song. Embrace it.

Starting in San Francisco, you will wind through the Golden State's most stunning scenery.

This trip launches from San Francisco. Here, indulge in the foodie town's culinary offerings, namely its stellar Asian cuisine. The legendary House of Nanking serves up traditional Chinese fare so delicious the line for a table sometimes stretches around the block. The wait is worth it though. The menu derives inspiration from the restaurant owner's years of watching expert chefs slice, sauté, stir, and fry in Shanghai food stalls. Consider overnighting at the elegantly appointed and decidedly urbane Palihotel before an early morning departure.

As soon as you untether from city limits, the countryside emerges, and the road leads to the Sierra Nevada. Spanning 400 miles (644 kilometers) across California, this region is home to snowy mountain peaks, deep canyons, and three impressive national parks: Yosemite, Sequoia, and Kings Canyon.

Of the three, Yosemite is the most popular, especially with hikers and backpackers. You can easily spend a week traversing trails to the granite monoliths, glacier-formed domes, and cascading waterfalls that make this park so iconic. If you opt to linger awhile, book lodging in advance at The Ahwahnee, a 1920s-era hotel nestled among Yosemite's famous rocks. If you

It's really quite astonishing that a state home to more people than Canada is also home to such unspoiled nature. Dive deep into it at Yosemite, Kings Canyon, and Sequoia National Parks, the latter of which is home to California's highest peak, Mount Whitney.

are short on time, stick to the sights in Yosemite Valley, such as the 620-foot (189-meter) Bridalveil Fall, whose plunging water sprays up a continual fine mist, or Half Dome, a rounded granite globe rising high in the sky and serving as the park's most notable landmark. There is also Yosemite Falls, three falls that morph together to form one of the highest waterfalls in the world.

Sequoia National Park and Kings Canyon National Park share a north-south border—and a claim to fame as the site of the oldest and tallest trees on the planet. Combined, these parks are larger than Yosemite but far less crowded. Take advantage of the solitude on a leisurely drive along the Kings Canyon Scenic Byway with its mountainous terrain and roadside pullouts with views galore. Then hike the easy trails to

the 1,700-year-old General Grant Tree, then pay a visit to the General Sherman Tree, the world's largest tree, measured by volume.

If you choose to spend the night, book a room at the family-friendly Montecito Sequoia Lodge or reserve a quaint timber cabin at Grant Grove Village within walking distance of the General Grant Tree. Don't leave without an upward gaze at Mount Whitney on the eastern edge of Sequoia National Park. At nearly 15,000 feet (4,572 meters), it is the highest peak in the continental United States and the southern terminus of the famous John Muir Trail.

From the sky-kissing peaks of Yosemite and the overpoweringly tall trees of Sequoia and Kings Canyon, go deep underground at Forestiere Underground Gardens. Considered →

From sandy beaches to snowcapped mountains, everywhere you look is a feast for the eyes. Stay in modern digs that are one with nature or a motel fit for movies. Either way, nature is at your doorstep.

→ one of Fresno's (literal) hidden gems, this labyrinth of subterranean rooms, courtyards, and passageways was constructed by Sicilian-born artist Baldassare Forestiere. Take a guided tour to see his underground masterpiece of grottos and patios filled with all manner of fruit trees: orange, grapefruit, kumquat, jujube, and pomegranate.

As you drive west, the craggy slopes of the Sierra Nevada smooth and soften into the wide, flat farmlands of central California. Before you know it, the air turns balmy and salty and the landscape lush. Then the sightline breaks open to reveal the glittering Pacific Ocean. You've reached San Simeon, and more importantly, California's enduring coastline along the Pacific Coast Highway (aka, State Route 1).

Perched on a bluff overlooking the pounding surf of San Simeon Bay sits Hearst Ranch Winery. This is an ideal spot to sample California-made wine and enjoy lunch (jackfruit street tacos, perhaps) in full view of the vineyard-dotted rolling hills.

Afterward, pair the winery visit with a tour of Hearst Castle. The history of the palatial estate once owned by famed American businessman and politician William Randolph Hearst dates back to 1865. That is when Hearst's father, George Hearst, bought the initial plot of land that would eventually become the 250,000-acre (101,171-hectare) Hearst Castle. Built between 1919 and 1947, the sprawling building features 165 rooms and displays Hearst's impressive art collection.

From San Simeon, the Pacific Coast Highway runs north, hugging the coastline all the way to Big Sur. This stretch of waterfront is some of the most spectacular in the world: clusters of enormous redwoods, wisps of drifting fog, and bluffs standing sentinel over whales that frolic in the ocean swells below. Drive slowly so as not to miss a thing.

In Big Sur, Pfeiffer Burns State Park offers plenty of nature hikes, including one leading to an 80-foot (24-meter) waterfall that spills onto a beachy cove. More gasp-worthy sights await at Bixby Bridge; if the span looks familiar, that's because it is. Bixby is a favorite setting for Hollywood filmmakers.

In town, grab dinner at Nepenthe. While the restaurant's steaks and seafood do not →

The further you venture from the coast, through the Sierra Nevada and towards the desert, the more it feels like you're traveling back in time. This is the California captured in Joan Didion's 1968 collection of essays, *Slouching Towards Bethlehem*.

→ disappoint, it is the panoramic ocean views that stand out. Ask for seats on the patio to truly experience the magic of Big Sur.

For lodging, there is the historic Deetjen's, a rustic but cozy inn, and for breakfast the next day, there is nothing like the heady aroma and mouthwatering flavors of the pastries at Big Sur Bakery. Think chocolate banana strudel, cinnamon rolls, and raisin danishes.

Skirting north, the Pacific Coast Highway connects to the charming seaside villages of Carmel-by-the-Sea and Monterey. In Carmel, stop by 5th Avenue Deli to pick up a picnic box (the Carmel Classic lunch includes the to-die-for espresso brownie), then head to Point Lobos State Natural Reserve to join a docent-led guided walk. This arresting setting not only shows off coves

and meadows but also one of the most diverse underwater habitats in the world. Keep your eyes open for seals, sea lions, otters, and migrating gray whales. If you miss spotting one of these in the wild, visit the Monterey Bay Aquarium. It sits right at the ocean's edge and was the first marine habitat to exhibit a living kelp forest.

California's natural wonders never cease to amaze, but that goes for its man-made attractions as well. As you leave the coast and curve north to the inland, check out The Mystery Spot in Santa Cruz. In events that seem to defy the laws of nature and gravity, such as balls that roll uphill or people leaning so far forward they should fall and yet don't, The Mystery Spot is a tilt-induced visual-illusion attraction. The tour guides might attribute it all to magic, but more than likely, it's

that the building's 20-degree angle causes misperceptions of the height and orientation of objects. Prepare to be wowed.

Then there's Devil's Slide Bunker south of your final destination of San Francisco. The bunker—a Second World War military observation station that once scanned for naval and aerial threats—teeters precariously on a slim rock outcropping. The crumbling remains cling to the summit, appearing as though they might plunge into the ocean at any minute. The story goes that a private owner nabbed the property after the military closed the station, scraping away the surrounding land for construction that never took place; hence, the structure's odd, and likely dangerous, perch. Snap photos for posterity from afar.

What's the best way to ease yourself back into the lively bustle of San Francisco? A laid-back stroll around Golden Gate Park. Then find a quiet corner table at French bistro Café Claude, a little spot perfect for recapping your big trip.

They say once you have experienced California's unrivaled beauty, you will feel a long-ing to return again and again. Perhaps to stand in the spray of Yosemite's waterfalls. Maybe to bask in the views of Mount Whitney or the enormous trunks of the Sierra Nevada sequoias. Definitely to soak up ocean views and to sink your toes in soft sand. The secret: with each return visit to the Golden State, the more California's natural wonders will start to feel like home. ◆

They say once you have experienced the bewitching appeal of California's unrivaled beauty, you will feel a longing to return again and again.

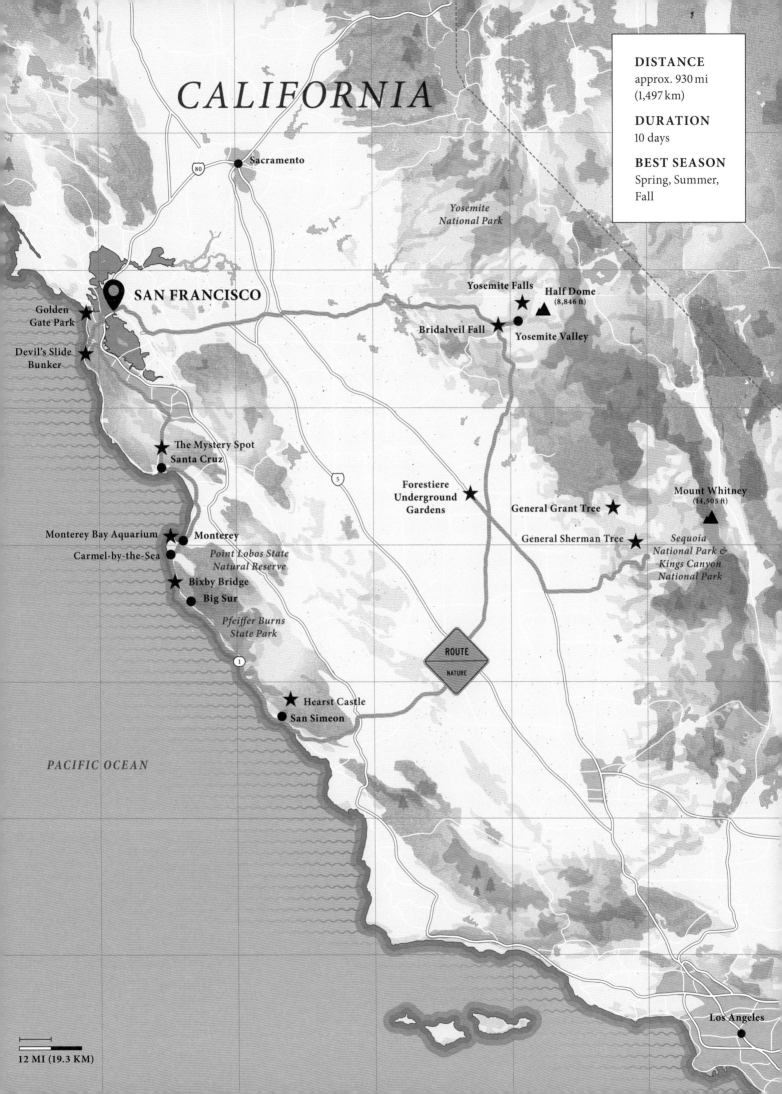

CALIFORNIA

DISTANCE
approx. 930 mi
(1,497 km)

DURATION
10 days

BEST SEASON
Spring, Summer,
Fall

Sacramento

*Yosemite
National Park*

★ SAN FRANCISCO

Yosemite Falls ★

Half Dome
(8,846 ft) ▲

Golden
Gate Park ★

Bridalveil Fall ★ ● Yosemite Valley

Devil's Slide
Bunker ★

★ The Mystery Spot
Santa Cruz ●

Forestiere
Underground ★
Gardens

Mount Whitney
(14,505 ft)

Monterey Bay Aquarium ★ ● Monterey

General Grant Tree ★

Carmel-by-the-Sea ●

*Point Lobos State
Natural Reserve*

General Sherman Tree ★

▲

★ Bixby Bridge

● Big Sur

*Sequoia
National Park &
Kings Canyon
National Park*

*Pfeiffer Burns
State Park*

①

ROUTE
━━━
NATURE

★ Hearst Castle
● San Simeon

PACIFIC OCEAN

Los Angeles ●

12 MI (19.3 KM)

Hang Ten on the 1: An Iconic Surf Route along the Pacific Coast Highway

BIG SUR, CALIFORNIA →
LOS ANGELES, CALIFORNIA

California State Route 1 has enchanted drivers for nearly a century. Now, it's your turn—with a surfboard in tow.

It doesn't get more California than the Pacific Coast Highway (PCH). For more than 600 miles (966 kilometers), this man-made masterpiece traverses dramatic cliffs, crashing coasts, and every hue of green and blue under the sun. It also serves as the gateway to some of America's best surf spots. So pack your board and embrace the #vanlife.

San Carpoforo Creek Beach is a widely beloved gem, with its best breaks at high tide.

The Californian coast has drawn surfers from around the world for decades—and for good reason. From hot spots like Santa Cruz and La Jolla to more secluded gems like San Simeon Point, there's plenty of break to go around.

No van? No problem. There's really no wrong way to travel the PCH as long as you commit at least 10 days to what will be an unforgettable road trip. Our route kicks off in Big Sur and ends roughly 300 miles (483 kilometers) down the coast, in Los Angeles. Feel free to extend it by starting in Santa Cruz and/or going all the way down to San Diego.

This being a book, we're duty bound to highlight Big Sur as a totem of American literati. Henry Miller, Jack Kerouac, Hunter S. Thompson, and Robinson Jeffers are just a few of the prestigious plenty who nested here. And while the magic of that era is in the rearview mirror, there's still plenty of life to be found at the Henry Miller Library, which is more of a performing arts center than a book repository.

Check the schedule of diverse cultural happenings or just swing by and see what you find.

You'll get your first glimpse of the Pacific's awesome ruggedness by pulling over at the Julia Pfeiffer Burns State Park Vista Point. Looking out toward rough waters and jagged rocks, this stretch of coast might not look exactly like a surfer's paradise. But that's not because spectacular surfing doesn't exist here—it's just tucked away. Andrew Molera Beach and Sand Dollar Beach are two such spots and can satisfy beginners and pros alike depending on the tide and time of day. The nearby Pfeiffer Big Sur Campground offers a fuss-free night under the redwoods while the Big Sur Lodge is a little more refined without feeling out of place. For something special in between, get your glamp on at Treebones Resort.

After a good night's sleep, it's on to more surfing. San Carpoforo Creek Beach is a widely beloved gem, with its best breaks at high tide, while more experienced surfers will find their fix on the epic waves at San Simeon Point a little further south. Both spots are excellent in February thanks to the mild winters—just don't forget to pack a wetsuit. Afterward, enjoy some fermented grapes at the Hearst Ranch Winery before refueling in the seaside village of Cambria (you can't go wrong at the Hidden Kitchen). Other highlights between San Carpoforo Creek and Cambria include many trailheads to fantastic hikes, the 147-year-old Piedras Blancas Light Station, and the Elephant Seal Vista Point, which is exactly what the name suggests. →

There's no wrong way to travel the PCH as long as you commit at least 10 days to what will be an unforgettable road trip.

From here to L. A.,
you'll pass through some
of California's
most storied surf
towns: Santa Barbara,
Ventura, Malibu,
Huntington Beach.

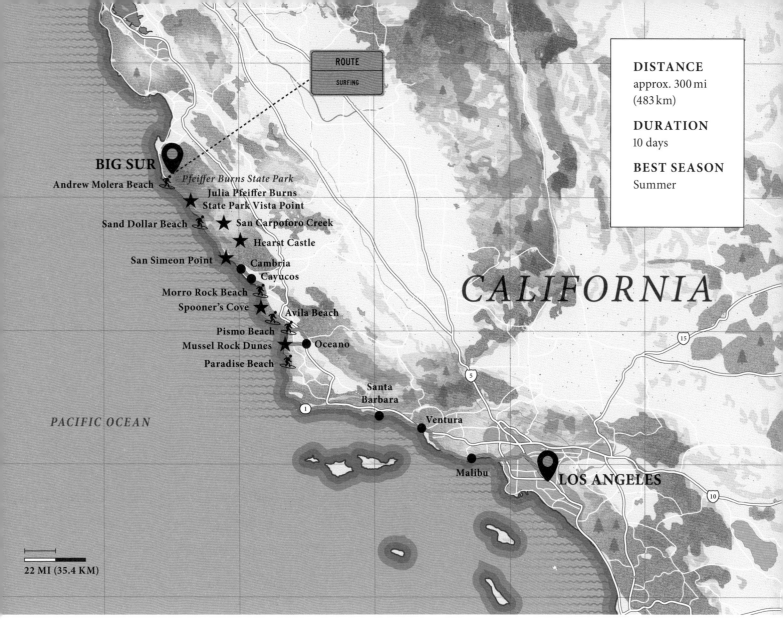

DISTANCE
approx. 300 mi
(483 km)

DURATION
10 days

BEST SEASON
Summer

BIG SUR

Andrew Molera Beach

Pfeiffer Burns State Park

Julia Pfeiffer Burns
State Park Vista Point

Sand Dollar Beach ★ San Carpoforo Creek

★ Hearst Castle

San Simeon Point

Cambria

Cayucos

Morro Rock Beach

Spooner's Cove

Avila Beach

Pismo Beach

Mussel Rock Dunes

Oceano

Paradise Beach

CALIFORNIA

PACIFIC OCEAN

Santa
Barbara

Ventura

Malibu

LOS ANGELES

ROUTE

SURFING

22 MI (35.4 KM)

The further south you head, the denser the crowds—and the warmer the
water. We like to start off on a rugged note up north before embracing the
laid-back atmosphere of surf towns like Santa Barbara, Ventura, Malibu,
and Huntington Beach.

→ Morro Rock Beach, about halfway to
L.A, is the next surfing hot spot en route. You'll
usually catch a clean break just a bit further
north—Cayucos comes highly recommended—
while the nature south of the main strip is just
plain beautiful to explore. Spooner's Cove will
take you away from the crowds and plant you
at the base of several majestic hikes. Get a full-
body workout by walking up to Hazard Peak
or Valencia Peak after a morning surf session.
Hard work is its own reward, as they say, and
so are the views. For a five-star sleep, check in
at the mountaintop Prefumo Crest Inn, an eco-
friendly ranch complete with open-air showers
and dreamy whirlpool tubs—just in case you
didn't get enough water at the ocean. It's worth
it if you're up for the splurge.

You'll find a more family-friendly scene
a little further down the coast at Avila Beach,
whose gentle waves are perfect for rookie surfers
and where there are enough amenities for those
who just want a day off the board. Grab a coffee
and pastry at Kraken or opt for some Hawaiian
shaved ice at Big Al's. When you've had enough
society for the day, dip into the hills and unwind
at the See Canyon Fruit Ranch or Kelsey See
Canyon Vineyards.

Eventually, you'll be ready to hit the
waves again, which you'll find in abundance at
Oceano. The ground swell is top-notch, and it'll
feel like you have the whole place to yourself, as
most of the crowds gather upcoast at Pismo Beach,
which is also great. Walking the Mussel Rock
Dunes is a must, as is a sunset at Paradise Beach.

From Oceano to L.A., you'll pass through
some of California's most storied surf towns:
Santa Barbara, Ventura, Malibu, Huntington
Beach. Each has its own special appeal and attracts surfers from around the world, which
means the waters could get crowded—just a
heads up to prepare for a change of pace. Fish
tacos are a rite of passage on this stretch; stand-
outs include Spencer Makenzie's in Ventura and
Sancho's Tacos in Huntington Beach. Meanwhile,
in Malibu, Neptune's Net is a seafood institution.
Really, though, there's so much to see and do
around here that to continue name-dropping
would be a futile endeavor. Besides, all the magic
happens between seeing and doing anyway. ◆

Straddle the Hana Highway along the Northeastern Coast of Maui

KAHULUI, MAUI → KAUPŌ, MAUI

With so much to see, planning the perfect itinerary will probably take longer than the drive itself.

By raw beauty, the Hana Highway may be unrivaled within these pages—or by any road trip on Earth, for that matter. While colloquially known as the "Road to Hana," the destination is merely an end to the means: towering coastal cliffs, plunging waterfalls, dense jungle, and panoramic views of the Pacific. You simply won't want it to be over.

The ride from Kipahulu to Hana and back is packed with more splendor than anyone could possibly marvel at.

All the one-lane bridges likely make the Hana Highway the slowest route in these pages. All the better, though, since that gives you plenty of time to take in the sights. Just don't forget to keep your eyes on the road while your head's on a swivel.

First things first: this drive is not for the queasy. With more than 600 hairpin curves, the Hana Highway is essentially one perpetual twist. Add to that nearly 60 single-lane bridges, and there's little room to take your eyes off the road. Don't worry, that's what the stops are for—and there are plenty. More on that in a moment. A convertible will furnish you with the quintessential Maui experience, though any car will do as long as it's relatively nimble. If you do opt for the open top, anytime between April and October will fetch you the best weather. Alas, in the rain, your Mustang may as well be a Focus.

At just over 50 miles (80 kilometers) long, the Hana Highway can be done in a day. But don't be fooled by the name: this is more of a paved path than a highway, with an average speed limit of around 25 mph (40 km/h). For day-trippers, it's best to give yourself between 10 and 12 hours, including sightseeing. A more laid-back itinerary would include a sleepover in Hana. That way, you can save some highlights for the way back and don't have to rush. The famed Hana-Maui Resort is a fantastic option if you're after a tropical paradise, while more budget-friendly lodging can be found at Hana Kai, the Bamboo Inn, or the Waiʻānapanapa State Park Cabins.

Hana Town is this road trip's most popular terminus and is revered for its "Old Hawaii" charm, thanks to its isolation from the forces of gentrification. Now, most car rental agencies will warn against driving too far past Hana—something about liability, etc., on unpaved roads. That said, the stretch between Hana and Kaupō, which bends around Maui's southeastern coast, is astonishing. Ask any local and they'll tell you the views are worth every bump and insurance void. (Truth be told—the road isn't *that* bad; a bit of dirt, a couple of divots). The 400-foot (122-meter) Waimoku Falls are a gem, as are the seven pools of the ʻOheʻo Gulch. You can even spend a night at the nearby Kīpahulu Campground in lieu of heading back to town. Other highlights of this so-called "no-man's-land" (there are still people around, though the crowds are considerably thinner) include Alelele Falls and Huialoha Church. Once you've come this far, you can decide whether to drive back through Hana or just drive full circle back to Kipahulu. →

The stretch between Hana and Kaupō, which bends around Maui's southeastern coast, is astonishing. Ask any local and they'll tell you the views are worth every bump and insurance void.

Walk through the lush rainforests and you'll understand why they're as cherished today as in ancient times.

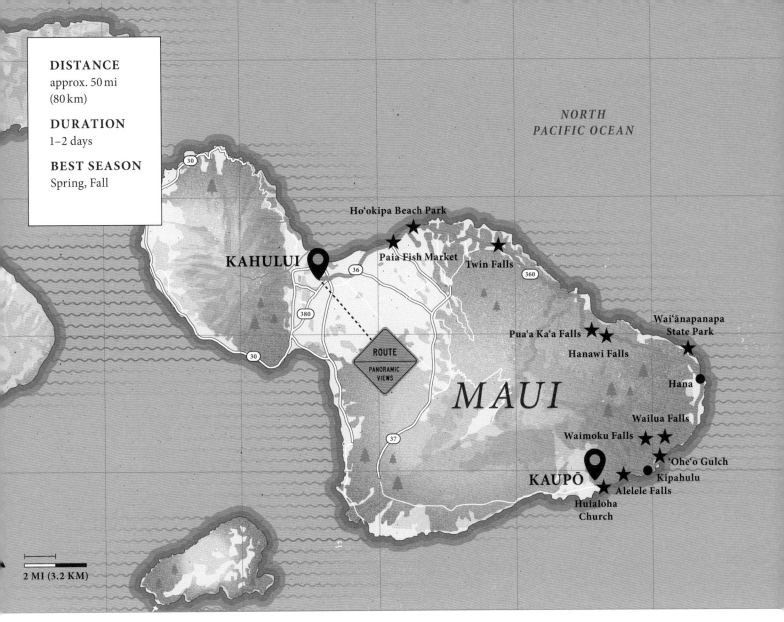

DISTANCE
approx. 50 mi
(80 km)

DURATION
1–2 days

BEST SEASON
Spring, Fall

NORTH
PACIFIC OCEAN

Ho'okipa Beach Park

Paia Fish Market

KAHULUI

Twin Falls

30

36

380

360

ROUTE
PANORAMIC
VIEWS

30

Pua'a Ka'a Falls

Hanawi Falls

Wai'ānapanapa
State Park

MAUI

Hana

37

Wailua Falls

Waimoku Falls

'Ohe'o Gulch

KAUPŌ

Kipahulu

Alelele Falls

Huialoha
Church

2 MI (3.2 KM)

Sandy beaches, lush jungle hikes, succulent fish tacos—where else can you get
all that within a stone's throw? Should the 50-mile (80-kilometer) route leave
you yearning for more, there's a whole other half of the island to explore.

→ Of course, this road trip has so much to offer that tail-end detours may not be necessary. The ride from Kipahulu to Hana and back is packed with more splendor than anyone could possibly marvel at. Ho'okipa Beach Park is a must, as is lunch at the nearby Mama's Fish House. If you're into chasing waterfalls, you'll find no shortage of options: Twin Falls, Pua'a Ka'a Falls, Wailua Falls, and Hanawi Falls are the main attractions. At the latter, the Wailua Iki Trail is perfect to get the legs moving. Really, though, you could pull over almost anywhere and find an unforgettable hike. Walk through the lush rainforests and you'll understand why they're as cherished today as in ancient times. If birds of paradise—both the winged and floral variety—are your calling, you'll have found

your heaven. As for drinks and dining, there are plenty of options all along the route. Just keep an eye out and drop into wherever looks promising.

Pull over almost anywhere and find an unforgettable hike.

Finally, for an end-of-day refresher, a dip at the black sand beach in Wai'anapanapa State Park is never a bad idea. There you can sleep under the stars at the campground or, if you're looking for something a little more luxe, the nearby Hana Estate is a worthy option.

On the way back, consider stopping just short of Kahului for a night at the Paia Inn. You'll be just steps from a pristine stretch of white sandy beach, not to mention right across from the Paia Fish Market in all its seafood glory. And if you feel like you missed something, you can always hit the road again tomorrow. ◆

303

The Great
American Road Trip

Roam the Roads From
Coast to Coast

This book was conceived by Aether Apparel and gestalten;
edited, and designed by gestalten

Edited by Robert Klanten, Florian Siebeck, and Elli Stühler
Contributing editors: Aether Apparel and Laura Austin

Introduction by Christian Näthler
Preface by Jonah Smith and Palmer West/Aether Apparel
Text by Jessica Dunham (pp. 32–43, 106–137, 198–217, 246–281),
Paul Oswell (pp. 16–25, 50–97, 138–161, 178–189, 218–245),
and Christian Näthler (pp. 8–15, 26–31, 44–49, 98–105, 162–177, 190–197, 282–301)
Captions by Christian Näthler
Copy edited by Jennifer Fratianni

Editorial Management by Anna Diekmann
Photo Editor: Madeline Dudley-Yates

Design, layout, and cover by Stefan Morgner

Map research by Anna Diekmann with assistance by Laura Austin and Florian Siebeck
Map design by Bureau Rabensteiner

Special thanks to Joel Wride and the extended Wride family, Davide Berruto, and Sari Tuschman

Typefaces: Minion by Robert Slimbach

Cover image by Hannah Armstrong/@hannahelizarmstrong/badtourist.co
Backcover image by Thinkstock/Getty Images

Printed by NINO Druck GmbH, Neustadt an der Weinstraße
Made in Germany

Published by gestalten, Berlin 2022
ISBN 978-3-96704-023-4

For more information, and to order books, please visit www.gestalten.com

Bibliographic information published by the Deutsche Nationalbibliothek.
The Deutsche Nationalbibliothek lists this publication in the Deutsche Nationalbibliografie;
detailed bibliographic data is available online at www.dnb.de

This book was printed on paper certified according to the standards of the FSC®.